How to Study

How to Study

a short introduction

Joan Turner

SAGE Publications
London • Thousand Oaks • New Delhi

© Joan Turner 2002

First published 2002

Apart from any fair dealing for the purposes of research or
private study, or criticism or review, as permitted under the
Copyright, Designs and Patents Act, 1988, this publication
may be reproduced, stored or transmitted in any form, or by
any means, only with the prior permission in writing of the
publishers, or in the case of reprographic reproduction, in
accordance with the terms of licences issued by the Copyright
Licensing Agency. Inquiries concerning reproduction outside
those terms should be sent to the publishers.

SAGE Publications Ltd
6 Bonhill Street
London EC2A 4PU

SAGE Publications Inc
2455 Teller Road
Thousand Oaks, California 91320

SAGE Publications India Pvt Ltd
32, M-Block Market
Greater Kailash - I
New Delhi 110 048

British Library Cataloguing in Publication data

A catalogue record for this book is available
from the British Library

ISBN 0 7619 6807 5
ISBN 0 7619 6808 3 (pbk)

Library of Congress Control Number: 2001132948

Typeset by SIVA Math Setters, Chennai, India
Printed in Great Britain by The Cromwell Press Ltd, Trowbridge, Wiltshire

Contents

Introductory Overview

WHO IS THIS BOOK FOR?

➤ You may have just left school and be in your first year at university.
➤ You may have started university after a gap year, or after having worked for a year or so.
➤ You may be what is known as a 'mature' student, which tends to mean anybody who has not gone to university straight after school, or after a gap year.
➤ You may be in the middle of your studies and feel that you could improve the way you're going about things.
➤ You may be on an access course, preparing yourself for university study in a particular subject or range of subjects.
➤ You may be in the sixth form, getting a sense of how best to prepare yourself for university study.
➤ You may be an international student wanting to know more about the academic culture and issues that affect students in Britain.
➤ You may be a university learning adviser or counsellor, a teacher of English for academic purposes, or schoolteacher, using the book as you see fit for discussion and awareness raising of relevant issues and skills development.

WHAT ARE THE AIMS OF THE BOOK?

I have four main aims in writing this book:

➤ to make you feel that, even if you're new to academic culture, you can develop within it;
➤ to take you behind the scenes of the study process and make you think about what is involved in the kinds of things you have to do;

> ➢ to build your confidence and your competence in a range of different tasks, whether it be writing, reading, or making the best use of your time;
> ➢ to help you make the most of your learning.

GETTING INTO ACADEMIC CULTURE

University life means many things and different things to different people. However, the academic side, as opposed to the social and the psychological, tends to have certain norms and values that are broadly taken for granted. These norms and values include:

> ➢ logical precision;
> ➢ being clear about what you're saying;
> ➢ accuracy in factual detail;
> ➢ accuracy in grammar and spelling;
> ➢ supporting your arguments;
> ➢ providing evidence for any claims you make;
> ➢ finding things out and documenting your sources.

You need to understand why you are asked to do the kinds of tasks you are asked to do and what they require. You need to know what your performance in those tasks is based on (see Chapter 4).

The process of getting into and understanding academic culture takes time. Even the most confident-seeming students have to go through a process of familiarisation, of finding out what's expected of them.

THE ASCERTAIN MODEL

Throughout the book, there will be occasional word-icons in the margin which highlight an active learning principle or good study strategy. Together the initial letters of these word icons make up the acronym ASCERTAIN. To ascertain means to find out and finding things out is the mark of the lifelong learner. The message is:

Once an active learner, always an active learner.

A is for actively seeking out information;
anticipating arguments, the content of a lecture, how to spend your time, the questions you might be asked in a seminar;
assimilating information;

analysing – breaking arguments down into their different dimensions and distinguishing between different points of view; asking questions, especially why? but also how? what? who? where? when?

S is for selecting from different sources, deciding what to take, what to leave, what to put in and what to leave out, what to spend more time on and what to spend less time on; summarising information; seeing things from different points of view; speaking in front of a group.

C is for classifying – identifying key analytical terms or concepts and grouping relevant information around them, for instance making mind maps, creating an orderly filing system for lecture notes and your own notes, and becoming familiar with the library classification system and where to get different kinds of information; being creative – making memorable notes, finding imaginative connections between ideas; being constructive – with your time, finding things you can usefully do, even in small amounts of time between different activities; being critical – not taking texts at face value, asking yourself questions as you read, standing back from your own feelings and looking at issues as they have been presented in the literature for your course; coping with and overcoming all sorts of difficulties – juggling family life with your studies, doing a part-time job, problems in your social life.

E is for evaluating or exercising judgement – learning how to distinguish between different kinds of information in the subject area, and taking up a stance having weighed up the available arguments; actively engaging with the ideas and arguments forming a topic within a discipline or course, and forming your own considered opinion; exploring – trying out new ways of doing things; effort, brainstorming to generate ideas, browsing in the library to get a wider view of the subject or subjects you are studying.

R is for reflecting on your learning and the study process – recognising that you could be doing things differently, that there are other approaches and attitudes that you might cultivate;

taking responsibility for your learning – taking a positive, pro-active approach to all aspects of your studies, and recognising that they are your responsibility, not your tutors';
taking risks – not being afraid to make mistakes;
trying out opinions or ideas even if you've unsure of them;
being rigorous – making sure you've got all the details right, in particular always checking your work and your sources.

T is for targeting – setting yourself goals and trying to meet them, thinking about purpose and the best way of achieving the specific purpose, revising selectively;
being thorough – carefully reading through any written work to make sure it is as clear as it can be, with no grammar or spelling mistakes, checking for details, such as when a book was written, documenting what you read;
transferring – transferring skills, abilities or understanding from one context to another.

A is for again! – doing things again, such as rereading, redrafting essays and looking again at what came under A at the beginning of this acronym!

I is for integrating information – restructuring how you thought about a topic or question in the light of new information on it, and continuously revising and consolidating what you know.

N is for negotiating and not being passive – negotiating an assignment deadline with your tutor if you're not going to make it, negotiating the meaning of texts by interrogating them and weighing them against other sources of information, methodological approaches and arguments.

Part One
BECOMING AN ACTIVE LEARNER

Nobody is ever completely prepared in advance for university life, and arguably it would not be good if you were. Going through university should be a transformative experience, making you a different person from the one you were before you began your studies. Being willing to go through the process of familiarisation with a new context, new ways of thinking, and new ways of doing things is perhaps the most important 'study skill' you should have, but you can develop a range of other skills and strategies which help you to make your way successfully through undergraduate study.

Studying is not just about learning particular content, whether in courses across one main subject area or in 'modules' from different subjects, it is also about actively managing the process of studying. To help you manage this process, the three chapters in this part of the book look at learning, memory, and time, respectively.

Chapter 1 helps you to reflect on the process of learning itself and gives you an insight into the various approaches and strategies that others adopt, what is generally effective, and what to avoid. Chapter 2 helps you to think about how you might best use your memory in learning, and introduces you to a range of mnemonic techniques. Chapter 3 encourages you to use your time wisely and shows how time and particular study strategies are interrelated.

The relationship between managing your learning and learning is symbiotic, the one feeds and nourishes the other. If you have a good learning experience, for example you work in a particular way on an essay writing task and you get a good result, you are likely to develop and refine that way of working. The same principle applies even if you get a bad result, only instead of refining, you change your way of working!

The important thing is that you reflect on what you're doing and take responsibility for what you learn and how you manage that learning.

1

Routes to Learning

warm-up exercise
Look at the following quotes from students. What do they have in common?

> I like to work through things, parrot-fashion.

> I was absolutely convinced I was doing things in the right way, but I got 43%.

> The more they [lecturers] do and the less you do is better. [Talking about getting handouts with lectures rather than taking own notes.]

> It's so easy to get off on the wrong track, you never really know what they want [talking about essay writing].

> In the oriental tradition, teachers take care of the students – very straight – to give advice, or to instruct – they don't digress. The British way is to say: 'oh, it's a very good idea ... but ...' – in a way they digress, it's not straightforward.

Discussion

All of the above quotes imply in one way or another that learning happens in a straight line. You move from one thing to the next, you learn 'parrot-fashion', as the first quote suggests, or there is a 'direct route' where you don't go 'off the track' or which is the 'right way' to do things. There is also a suggestion of a direct link between the tutor and the student. What the tutor teaches, the student learns, as if the tutor were handing over a piece of cake which the student ate. The first four quotes are from British students, but the last one comes from a Korean student. It is often seen as a cultural difference that western education is more 'learner-centred' while East Asian education is teacher-dominated. While this is broadly true and has much wider ramifications than discussed here, we see from the above examples that assumptions from at least some 'western' students' viewpoints are that they will get 'handouts', both literally and metaphorically, from the teacher. Such a viewpoint does not seem to involve the active engagement of the learner. The student is just a passive receptacle for the teacher's or the textbook's knowledge, or a parrot!

LEARNING IS A JOURNEY

Much of the above discussion can be related to the concept of a journey. Is the student responsible for mapping out her/his own route through university, or should the way be already paved by the tutor? The concept of a journey underlies life itself. We go through life and we experience all kinds of things along the way. Similarly, we talk about 'going through' university. Going through university is like a stage in life. For some people it happens after school and before 'the rest of life'. For others it will happen later in life, after a few years of working perhaps, or after having children, or after losing a job and looking for a different kind of job by getting different or higher qualifications.

For whatever reason you set off on a university degree, it is as if you're going on a journey. Sometimes you will feel that you are sauntering along, taking everything in your stride, while at other times you will be very much aware that you're on a steep learning curve. The learning process is not smooth – its pace varies, as does the amount of effort and energy needed.

The mental journey of getting a university degree requires:

➢ a great deal of practical organisation as you go along;
➢ the mental flexibility to get round obstacles and cope with a wide range of social, psychological and intellectual challenges;
➢ the mental (and physical) stamina to stay on course.

Some elements of the university journey are well known in advance, while others are unknown. The fact that you progress through the university system means that you have to meet certain requirements at each stage. Every degree programme is different, but that kind of information will be mapped out in advance. This means that you will know things like the number of courses or modules that you can take in a year, the range that you can choose from, the number of assignments you have to do for each and how much each assignment is worth. In some universities, you can choose between different pathways through your degree, where you have quite a wide choice of modules in different subject areas, while in others you follow different aspects of the same subject, some of which are compulsory and some of which are optional.

You will also need to know such things as the ratio of assessed course work to end-of-year exams, and the weighting of assignments relative to each other and to the year in which they are undertaken. For example, some examination administrators talk about 'exit velocity', which means that the courses you take in your final year are worth more than those in your first year. There is therefore usually a hierarchical progression of difficulty and value to the courses you do each year.

All of this information is mapped out in course handbooks or student guides, which you will probably be given in your first week or so at university. As you receive a lot of information at this time, it is essential that you don't put such guides away and forget all about them, but have them ready to hand for quick reference. They are a bit like physical maps through the assessment system, telling you what you need at each stage in order to graduate.

Finding your Way Around the Subject Landscape

Even if you have begun to study at school the subject or subjects you're studying at university, you are always going to be a relative newcomer to that field of study. However, the field itself has already been extensively researched and therefore a number of maps of what it looks like will already have been drawn, as it were. Of course, I'm not talking about the kind of maps that you can buy in the shops to help you find your way round a strange town – I'm talking about conceptual maps. The various questions that have been asked in the past will have generated a lot of literature, which in turn will have been distilled in the various textbooks that you have on your reading lists. Nowadays, most questions that are asked in different fields of study are also approached from different theoretical perspectives.

It is these perspectives that you will have to become aware of as well as how the different kinds of information that are available fit into them. This is a bit like trying to find your way around a very complex map – not of places, but of arguments, people, and methodological approaches.

You may be like an explorer going into uncharted territory, but the territory itself is already mapped out (see also the discussion in Chapter 9 on finding your own academic voice).

My viewpoint throughout this book is that you should take charge of your own learning, think for yourself, and be prepared to work hard. However, as the quotes at the beginning of this chapter show, it is not always easy to do. You have to work at taking charge of your learning in the same way as you have to work at understanding the topics you are studying. It is not simply a question of having a natural academic ability and applying it – it is a question of finding and developing strategies for working in an academic way. Even if you feel you are relatively new to academic culture, you can develop within it.

THE STUDENT AS INDEPENDENT LEARNER

The issue of taking responsibility for your own learning is one that educationists discuss a lot, and the general consensus in the British educational context is that it is a good thing, not least because it is likely to achieve better outcomes, such as higher marks and a better overall degree.

TAKING RESPONSIBILITY FOR YOUR OWN LEARNING

My viewpoint on your learning journey is that you should be responsible for the route it takes in terms of what you have achieved by the end of your studies. This means thinking for yourself and being responsible for what you learn. Ultimately, you will create your own mental maps of your understanding in the topics that you study. You can think of these as mind maps (see Chapter 2) which will change as your understanding and breadth of knowledge on a topic increases.

Taking responsibility for your learning is supported in the following quotes from two established academics:

> ➤ A seminar leader is not supposed to program her students to share her views but to lead discussion. The quality of the discussion depends not on the leader but on the students. It is not the seminar leader's job to fire students with enthusiasm: if they do not have that already, they shouldn't be there.
>
> (Germaine Greer, *The Independent*, 19 October 2000, Education section)

> ➤ He wanted to show us that thinking for oneself was what mattered, not showing the 'correct' things.
> ➤ He told us about a candidate's essay: 'I disagreed with every word of it, so I gave it 100 percent.'
>
> (Christopher Hill on his former tutor at Oxford University, *Times Higher Education Supplement*, 16 December 1994)

These quotes take the spotlight off the tutors in the study process and put it on the individual student. Basically, they suggest that it is the attitudes you bring with you to university that determine how much you get out of it. If you want to find things out, have a questioning attitude, are prepared to think for yourself, you should do well.

ascertain

A

ask questions

ascertain

E

explore possible answers

ACTION!   If you don't already have it, cultivate an attitude of intellectual curiosity!

ascertain

R

reflect

APPROACHES TO LEARNING

Taking responsibility for your learning does not just apply to conceptual knowledge. It applies also to how you manage the study process. Learning does not happen simply by dint of natural academic ability, which you either have or have not, learning at university is also a social process. It takes place in an institutional context which has its own norms and ways of going about things. For example, you will probably have to write essays, which is not something you have to do in everyday life (see Chapter 5). You may feel relatively new to academic culture and it might take you some time to get used to its ways of working, but you can do so. You need to find and develop strategies for working and learning within it.

In this section, I shall look at different approaches to and different aspects of the learning process so that you can become aware of different attitudes towards learning and different ways of going about things, which you might then try out for yourself.

There are no magic tips, and no one way that guarantees success in your studies, but you may find there are changes you can make to your way of working or to your attitude towards your studies that help you to become a more effective learner.

Deep-holistic and Surface-atomistic Learners

Some researchers in Britain and Sweden have identified what they call 'deep-holistic' and 'surface-atomistic' learners (Marton et al., 1984). The researchers arrived at those rather unwieldy descriptions after recorded discussions with students, where they talked about how they approached different aspects of their studies. Some of the research was based on the analysis of essays and what students said about how they went about writing them.

TASK 1.1

Read the following descriptions of student attitudes and approaches. Can you guess which descriptions fit a deep-holistic learner, and which fit a surface-atomistic learner?

Description	Deep-holistic learners	Surface-atomistic learners
Make sure they fully understand concepts, ideas, and the relationships between them		
Focus more on reproducing what they think should be learnt rather than on fully understanding it		

Take what they read or hear at face value and attempt to memorise it		
Fit what they are working on into an overall framework, e.g. being aware that author X is taking theoretical perspective Y and disagrees with some of the arguments of Z, rather than just taking what X writes at face value		
Tend to see learning as the accumulation of individual facts, and don't always connect them to specific situations		
Have an inquiring, questioning attitude to what they are reading about/listening to, rather than an absorption, accepting, approach		
Think of what they learn as something completely separate from them rather than as something that can change the way they think or how they see things		
Integrate new understanding into their existing conception of an area of study, e.g. they don't go into a topic as if their mind were a blank slate, they try to think of what kinds of issues the topic deals with before they read about it		

TASK 1.2

Discuss with friends which descriptions you identify with, which are definitely not you, and which you might like to try out. The solution to task 1.1 can be found at the end of the chapter.

Discussion

Given the evaluative connotations in English of the words 'deep' and 'surface', the approach of deep-holistic learners would appear to be more highly valued. The attitudes associated with their approach also tie in with what was said above about being active learners. They appear to take responsibility for their learning by being more in control of the study process overall.

The strategies advocated for managing your assignments in Chapter 2 may be said to conform to the deep-holistic approach to learning. They are deep-holistic because they require you to:

➢ rely on your own understanding of the material you are working with;
➢ relate your work to the purpose of an assignment, for example, keep it within the framework of the title set for an essay;
➢ organise the whole assignment in a coherent and consistent fashion.

Making notes by copying down sentences exactly as they are written in a textbook, however, could be indicative of a surface-atomistic approach whereby you are doing something mechanically, hoping that it stays in your memory rather than actively engaging with the ideas in the text, and trying to see things the way the writer was seeing them.

As will be mentioned in Chapter 3, such a strategy is not the most productive use of your time. Time is better spent actually thinking about what you are reading, processing the information as it were, asking yourself questions about it and how it relates to other aspects of the subject.

Choosing the Approach and the Strategy to Suit the Circumstances

The usefulness of the approach to learning is also determined by the tasks that have to be carried out. Some tasks may be better performed by an approach that is more surface-atomistic in orientation. For example, in cases where you are tested on the precise definitions of things, as in some multiple-choice tasks, it is better to memorise those definitions in order to be able to reproduce them.

In the case of taking care over spelling (see Chapter 10), the detailed precision required here might be labelled surface-atomistic, as it is focusing on words rather than the meaning behind the words. However, as discussed in Chapter 10, this is nonetheless necessary. The approaches can therefore be best evaluated in relation to tasks rather than as absolutes.

Organisational Strategies and Attitude in the Study Process

You need to have strategies for practical organisation. These might include systems to help with note-taking and filing which are at the same time linked to learning (see Chapters 2 and 4 for examples) or routines of time management (Chapter 3) and strategies for revision (Chapter 8).

You need a positive and constructive attitude towards change – both conceptual change where you might have to shift your position on certain issues or ideas, and changes in the things that you have to deal with from day to day. You meet new ideas, new challenges, and new people.

Your learning happens on different levels, on the level of understanding a range of different subject content, on the level of how you interact both with texts and people, and on the level of meeting institutional requirements. All of these levels interrelate in the study process, but you will sometimes have to prioritise one over the others.

Your judgement over what to prioritise and when is something else that you need to develop as you go through your programme of study.

You also have to be prepared to put a lot of effort into things you possibly find difficult or time-consuming, as well as disciplining yourself to make sure you do what you have to do. You may occasionally have to conjure up some enthusiasm where none is there naturally. The point is that your attitude both towards learning and towards how you learn is important.

Operating Strategically

> The main purpose of universities is to provide students with an excuse to pass the time for 3 years.
>
> (The playwright David Mamet, from an interview in the *Times Higher Education Supplement*, 3 March 2000)

This rather sour note about university education stems from the American playwright's critical position on how English literature is being taught at universities in the United States. His view is that literature teaching 'distances kids from any possible enjoyment of literature'.

That there can be a conflict between what a university education purports to achieve – a really worthwhile learning experience, valuable for its own sake – and the reality of the situation, has been evident for some time. One of the ways it comes up is in the notion of 'strategic' learners. So-called 'strategic learners' are those who see studying as a 'game'. This means they find out the rules of how the 'degree game' works, and channel their energies into that, rather than into enhancing their own learning experience. This attitude has been identified by, for example, Entwistle and Wilson (1977), and is also apparent in the examination 'game' played particularly well by some students getting good degrees, which is discussed in Chapter 8 on examinations.

The 'game' approach to getting a degree makes it appear much more a question of jumping through hoops than really getting to grips with learning. However, managing the study process does also require that you know what the hoops are.

TASK 1.3

What do you think of the following attitudes and strategies? Will they work, do you think? Discuss with other students.

1   Working only for those assignments that are worth a lot of marks in the overall breakdown of what counts towards your degree, and deliberately not doing much for others.
2   Writing what you think the individual tutor who has set the work wants or will like, in order to get a better mark.
3   Making sure you quote from published work by your tutor, in the hope of getting a better mark.

4   Putting a lot of effort into finding out what's likely to come up in the exams in order to concentrate only on those topics (see Chapter 8).
5   Choosing courses or modules because you've heard that it's easier to get higher marks in them than in others.
6   Making a special effort to get yourself noticed in class – for example, always saying something in every seminar, because you believe that if you make a good impression on a lecturer, you'll get a higher mark.

Striking a Balance

Obviously, I'm not going to advocate that you should behave as in the above quotes, because I believe you'll get a lot more out of your studies if you actually want to know things and understand how people have come to think the way they do about things, rather than trying to manipulate the system. However, I don't think either that you should naively follow your courses without thinking about where they're leading and how they fit into the overall scheme of your degree.

Paying attention to the regulatory or procedural aspects of your course is important as I mentioned in the section above on what is mapped out for you in your studies. You should take account of how much an assignment is worth when managing the amount of time you spend on it.

You may have to put to one side your particular interest in a topic if that topic does not play a major role in the overall course. To some extent, this goes against the grain of being the enthusiastic, motivated, independently learning student that was highlighted in the quotes from academics above, but sometimes you need to strike a balance between your enthusiasms and the need to follow course requirements.

The main thing is that you are aware of all the competing demands on you as a student so that you can both manage the study process and reach a deeper understanding and level of insight into the subject or subjects you are studying.

You need the motivation to learn, the patience to find out the best ways of learning for you, and the willingness to change both your approach and your attitude to learning, if required. It is my belief that you can become a more effective learner, but the process won't happen overnight. Giving some thought to how you approach your learning, how it differs from others, and the kinds of results you achieve is a first step in this process.

Issues of Confidence

> Initially I felt surrounded by people who seemed cleverer and better educated than me. I now know this is a common experience. You quickly learn that overbearing self-esteem does not translate itself into good exam marks, though!

This was the reply the journalist and foreign correspondent, Allan Little, gave to the question: What is your worst memory of university? Later in the interview, he says:

> among your classmates, don't think the ones with the most self-confidence are necessarily the brightest.
> (in *EdiT*, The University of Edinburgh Magazine, Volume 2, 2, 2000)

Often students do make the mistake of thinking that the most confident-seeming students are the best students. However, personal confidence is not the same as study confidence. Study confidence comes from being in control over your own learning. This means being clear about your goals, or even trying to become clear about your goals, as they probably won't at first be clear in all aspects of the study process.

It's important to remember that everybody experiences lack of confidence about some aspects of their lives, especially when they are tackling something new. A lot of students lack confidence at the beginning of their studies. The familiarisation process takes time and experience, and confidence builds gradually. This is why it's important to think about how you are actually going about things rather than just taking things as they come. Don't just hand in an essay, for example, and hope for the best.

Don't undermine your own confidence by telling yourself things such as the following: 'Oh, I'll never get through this'; 'I'm not the type to be able to do this'; 'This isn't for me'; 'My tutor doesn't like me'; 'My tutor's got it in for me'. These kinds of statements are called 'negative self-reports' (see also Chapter 8) – and as the term suggests, you're telling yourself you're no good. And if you're telling yourself you're no good, well … what do you expect?

Uncharted Territory

Learning is not a straightforward process. Your route through your degree is unlikely to be completely smooth. While the subject matter you study comes from well-worn paths of learning, your own learning, the inner journey that you yourself will make, is uncharted territory. You are the one who will map it out.

Only you can do your learning!

SUMMARY

Your journey through university involves:

➢ practically managing your studies;
➢ personally engaging with the ideas, theories, processes and procedures that structure the subjects or modules you're studying;
➢ strategically managing your studies in order to get the best results from your efforts;
➢ reflecting on how you learn and how to manage your studies in order to improve both;
➢ building your confidence as you go along.

SOLUTION TO TASK 1.1

Deep-holistic learners are students who:	*Surface-atomistic learners* are students who:
➤ Make sure they fully understand concepts, ideas, and the relationships between them.	➤ Take what they read or hear at face value and attempt to store it.
➤ Fit what they are working on into an overall framework, e.g. being aware that author X is taking theoretical perspective Y and disagrees with some of the arguments of Z, rather than just taking what X writes at face value.	➤ Tend to see learning as the accumulation of individual facts, and don't always connect them to specific situations.
➤ Have an inquiring, questioning attitude to what they are reading about/listening to, rather than an absorption, accepting, approach.	➤ Think of what they learn as something completely separate from them rather than as something that can change the way they think or how they see things.
➤ Integrate new understanding into their existing conception of an area of study, e.g. they don't go into a topic as if their mind were a blank slate, they try to think of what kinds of issues the topic deals with before they read about it.	➤ Focus more on reproducing what they think should be learnt rather than on fully understanding it.

2

Learning to Remember

What strikes you about the following quotes?

> I've got the memory span of a fish. One load has to depart before I can take anything else in.

> I don't have long-term memory.

> I can do a really good essay and get 65% but can never remember what I did.

> I've got a fantastic memory for names and faces but can never remember anything that's in my textbooks.

Discussion

All of the above quotes are exaggerated and couldn't – strictly speaking – be true. However, they point up a link between studying and remembering and suggest that there is a certain amount of anxiety associated with being able to remember things. The fact that the students making the quotes are also making negative comments about themselves also points to a self-deprecating tendency which is quite common among students, not only when discussing their ability to remember things but also when talking about their studies in general. There can be a peer group ethos that dictates you should be disorganised, scatty, more focused on your social life than your studies. By not being too clever or too organised, by not being the 'ideal' student as it were, you have more chance perhaps of being popular. Student life is full of conflicts, and it is perhaps not surprising that the human faculty of memory is one of the areas on which anxieties are focused as it represents both the striving for perfection and the difficulties of achieving it. The aim of this chapter is to show you that there are ways in which you can improve your memory and your methods of learning at the same time.

THE ART OF MEMORY

The art of memory was one of the oldest arts taught in western education. By 'western' education I mean that going back to ancient Greece, more than 2000 years ago. Extremely elaborate ways of remembering were taught in conjunction with the art of oratory, namely giving long and persuasive speeches in the promotion or defence of some cause. The subject taught was called rhetoric, and memory was one of its five parts. The other parts, relating to gathering and selecting information to put forward in an argument and how best to put the parts of the argument together, are not that dissimilar to the basic principles of essay writing today except that they related to long speeches rather than writing and therefore depended much more on memory.

In her book, *The Art of Memory*, Yates (1969: 3) talks of the 'mnemonic gymnastics' of the ancient orators as they practised their architectural system of remembering things. A mnemonic can be anything that helps you to remember something. The orators' training in the techniques of the art of memory involved imagining a coherent system of 'places', such as the rooms and the parts of rooms in a building, putting images in each of these places and associating those images with specific things, such as ideas, arguments or particular phrasings of words. The images they used included such things as anchors and weapons, which would have had strong resonance with the times when Greece – or the state of Athens as it was then – was constantly fighting battles at sea. Each element of the speech which the orator would have to make would then be associated with one of these images and the place in which it was located. Then, while making his speech, the orator would move through his building in his imagination, ensuring he got everything in the right order.

The system, once thoroughly thought out and committed to memory by rehearsing and re-rehearsing it, could be used again and again for different kinds of information at different times.

Memory and Technology

Over time the cultural need for such elaborate systems of remembering has lessened, as the technological resources available to take the burden off individual human memory have increased. The art of memory arose at a time when speech was the primary means of communication. An increase in the use of written language meant that information could be stored and retrieved at different times so that there was no longer the same need for reliance on individual memory. The printing press and then more recently the computer and the internet have arguably all taken the strain off the need to remember an extended number of things.

On the other hand, the range of types of information that the contemporary individual has to deal with has vastly increased. This means that our memory for things extends beyond that which we have actually experienced at first hand. For example, the early cinema technology of silent films is something that most people still alive today will not have experienced as a 'going out' experience. However, we may still have seen the images of silent films on television, and feel that we have experienced them.

Recording technology gives us access to the history of television and radio so that we not only have 'information' in a cognitive sense which we store in our minds, but also visual images and sound images which provide access to the look and sound of a decade whether or not we actually 'remember' that decade. Our own personal memory of things is therefore widened by our interaction with technology.

The multitudinous resources of technology and the access it provides to an array of 'information' can make learning both easier and more difficult. Easy access to information can cut down the time it takes to find it, for example. However, we also have to process more kinds of information – visual, verbal, cultural and social – and sort out the connections between them in more complex ways.

While the practice of teaching students to construct elaborate imaginary spaces in the mind in order to train the memory is no longer a feature of twenty-first-century education, the principles of storage and retrieval on which these elaborate systems were based remain relevant.

THE MIND IS A CONTAINER

Talking of *storage* and *retrieval* relates perhaps more to computers than to our minds, although we also say things like 'it's all *in* the mind' or 'I have to get it *into* my head that …', which suggests that we think of both computers and our minds as containers. Computers have large storage capacity and can retrieve things quickly. In the study context, it can also be helpful to use the storage and retrieval metaphor to think about how we *record* information so that it helps us to *retrieve* it when we need it.

Without thinking about it, we 'store' memories in different ways. We have, as it were, different access routes into the mind. The next section will look at some of these different access routes and discuss some ways in which they might be deliberately used to help you remember what you want or need to remember.

Routes to Remembering

We have all had what we think of as 'unforgettable' experiences. We all also have what might be termed 'quirky' memories – facts, situations, places, smells, that we always remember, whether or not they are important or otherwise relevant to our lives. For example, the French novelist Proust wrote an extremely long novel, entitled *In Search of Time Past*, which was triggered by his memory of the smell of cakes called *madeleines*. The sense of smell may not be particularly helpful for remembering things in the study context (although you may be able to think of instances), but all of our senses can be involved in what makes something memorable. I want to look at visual impact, sound, the emotions, and what is known as episodic memory as ways of remembering which you can deliberately convert into making things that you want to learn more memorable.

Visual Impact

Visual impact can be very forceful. For example, seeing somebody at a wedding wearing an exotic hat with birds and butterflies on it can make you visualise that hat every time you see the person. You might have a 'love at first sight' experience when you see someone strikingly handsome or beautiful. Striking colours, unusual juxtapositions, something that stands out because it is surrounded by shade can all be memorable. For you, such an experience of memorability is natural, even though the effect could have been contrived. This is the sort of thing that advertisers are extremely good at.

TASK 2.1

Think of a current advertisement that you find particularly striking. What is it that makes it striking? Compare with friends whether they find the same ad striking, and for the same reasons.

Creating Visual Impact

Visual impact to make something memorable can be contrived in very simple ways. For example, you might want to write all your notes for one particular lecture course on yellow paper rather than the more normal white paper. It can help you to recall what you've written by remembering how the words look against the yellow background. Using such simple things as bullet points visually can also make an impact. For example, in researching arguments for and against on a particular issue, you could use rounded bullet points in red ink for information that supported the argument, and diamond shapes in black ink for information that supported the argument against. You could remember the system itself by remembering *r* for *red* and *round* in the case of for arguments, and black as the negative emotion for contra arguments. If you adhered to this system for every assignment, it would soon become second nature, as their architectural system of places did for the ancient orators.

The Mind Map

Mind maps also can have a very strong visual impact especially when colour, capital letters and different sizes of writing are used to organise a whole landscape of issues, arguments and facts.

The use of the mind map has been made more popular in recent years by Tony Buzan (1981, 1982, 1986), whose work also owes a debt to the historical work of Frances Yates and in particular her research into the art of memory during the Renaissance. The Renaissance scholar, Giulio Camillo, for example, created what was called a 'memory theatre', an extremely elaborate and complex system of detailed knowledge, arranged in the shape of an ancient Greek or Roman amphitheatre. This theatre had seven gates or entrances, and seven tiers, in association with the biblical Solomon's seven pillars of wisdom. In tune with Renaissance times, he was intending to 'map' the whole of knowledge and record it for posterity.

A mind map that you might create would not need to be so elaborate, but could nonetheless be helpful to you during revision, or in generally helping you to get an overview of a particular field of study. It is something that you could work on deliberately to help you to integrate different strands of thought on any one topic. Dividing an area of study up into its relevant strands is in any case a useful exercise in analysis, quite apart from the benefits of the layout of the map, helping you to remember the content.

Figure 2.1 shows a very simple mind map of the different meanings and associations that the word 'exploitation' taps into or gives rise to.

TASK 2.2

Make a similar mind map of a concept or topic that you are currently working on as part of your studies.

Association by Images

Meanings or concepts that you have difficulty remembering can also be made more memorable by association with a visual image. This is a technique often used in foreign language teaching, where you need to remember a lot of new and unfamiliar words. The following is an example of a visual image which might help a student of English as a foreign language to remember the colloquial word 'cram' as in cramming for an exam.

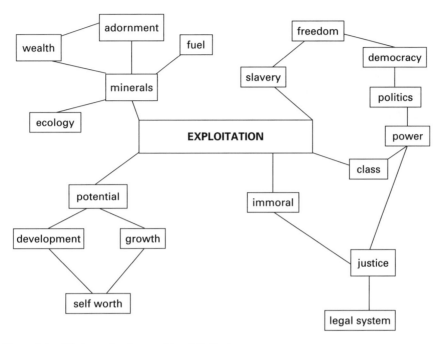

Figure 2.1 *Mind map for the word 'exploitation'*

The image of the party shoe is associated with the fairy story of Cinderella. As this fairy tale is known world-wide, the significance of the shoe will be well known too. Whoever's foot fits the shoe will marry the prince. The comedy of the ugly sisters trying to 'cram' their feet into it is memorable, and so the image of a shoe and the word 'cram' can be a memorable association.

Creating associative links can help also with distinguishing between the spellings and meanings of same-sounding words. Take the words *compliment* and *complement*, which are pronounced in exactly the same way but have different meanings and only one letter different in the way they are spelt. One has an *i* in the middle while the other has an *e*. Remembering them in phrases or sentences which make the meaning clear and also have some other feature which highlights the 'i' or 'e' is a way of helping you to remember which one is which. Here are two possible such sayings: fishing for compliments; and the asparagus complements the fish nicely.

In the phrase 'fishing for compliments', there are two 'i's in fishing, and the 'i' sound is dominant, so that helps you to remember that kind of compliment, which you 'pay' somebody as well as 'fish for'. The other sentence gives a context where the lesser used word 'complement' occurs, namely when talking about food. When one kind of food *goes well with* or *completes* another kind of food, we use *complement* with an *e*. In this sentence, there is only one 'i' in fish, and the letter i is otherwise not dominant. Another way of remembering the 'e' is to relate it to one way of explaining the meaning of complement, namely to comple*te* something.

Remembering things by setting up a strong association need not be restricted to single words or meanings, but can be transferred to any learning context. If you're a doodler, for example, make your doodles mnemonic! This means associating your doodles with whatever you're doodling to! The images you make can be as grotesque, way out, or imaginative as you like. The link only needs to be memorable to you!

Sound Links

Sound is another feature that can stand out. How many films do you remember because of their soundtrack? Something that is extra loud makes an impact, even if it is only memorable because you want to forget it! Variation in sound usually holds the attention for a longer time-span than something which drones on with no variation. Think of those lecturers whose voice carries and where certain things are stressed, as opposed to someone who perhaps mumbles or reads from something written down, without giving full attention to what is being said. Whose lecture is more memorable?

Although listening to music while studying is not a strategy I would advocate, if you do have to do it, at least make a point of linking what you're listening to to what you're studying. Then, at a later date, you can say to yourself 'Oh, that was the bit I was reading when I was listening to my favourite track on X's album'. The hope is that you remember what you were studying as well as the track!

The Emotions

More emotive factors such as anger, horror, ugliness, shock and surprise also make a strong impact on memory. For example, in the Middle Ages the use of grotesque images became very widespread and was intended to remind people of the horrors of hell and deter them from wrongdoing, or from straying from the path of religious teaching.

Many of these images can still be seen as gargoyles on medieval European cathedrals, although their function as 'reminders' has of course gone.

In the case of your own studies, the extent to which you get personally involved with a topic can also make the ideas or analytical concepts it entails more memorable. You don't have to treat what you're studying as something completely alien to you, something that you keep at a distance – you can make it meaningful to you in a more personal way. Many people are familiar with the experience of being caught up in the enthusiasm of a teacher or lecturer who obviously feels passionate about their subject. You need not only be the recipient of passionate enthusiasm, however – you can create it for yourself. For example, you could imagine yourself actually in a particular context, whether it be as a spectator in the audience of a play put on in the seventeenth century or as setting up your own small business. This might help you think more clearly and more widely on the issues concerned and also make them more memorable.

Becoming personally involved in a topic can be a good way of helping you to understand things more deeply. Also, you don't always have to wait for something that you find intellectually stimulating – you can, if you try, find enthusiasm for any topic!

ascertain

E

engage

CULTIVATING EPISODIC MEMORY

Where Were You When ...?

The ability of people to remember exactly what they were doing at the time of horrific events is well known. The assassination of John Kennedy, the president of the United States, in 1963 is one such event. Many people remember exactly what they were doing when they heard the news. The assassination of John Lennon in 1980 was another tragic event that struck people so forcefully that they can still clearly remember how it infiltrated their own lives. The setting up of strong associations with particular events is known as *episodic memory*.

Episodic memory applies in more mundane situations as well. You might, for example, be familiar with the context of going into a room and forgetting what you had gone in there for. You have to take yourself back to what you were doing beforehand in order to 'relive' the situation that prompted you to go into the room in the first place. Similar ways of using the memory can be employed with witnesses in traffic accidents. They might be asked to take themselves back to what they were doing before the accident happened in order to trigger their memory of what happened in greater detail. They might be encouraged to recount any detail that they remember of the scene, such as the weather, how many people were around, what they were thinking about, so that they might remember something they observed without realising that they had observed it.

You can cultivate your own episodic memory by remembering the setting in which you heard, saw, or even just thought about something as well as the actual content. In the context of your studies, attending a lecture for example, you could make a point of noting your surroundings as well as concentrating on the lecture. So you might remember that in X's lecture on the subject of Y, one that you're particularly interested in, or need to get to grips with, it was a bright sunny day, or a dull, rainy day, whatever the case may be. You were also sitting next to B who was scribbling away furiously. You of course were *not* trying to record everything as that would be counter-productive, and is not possible in any case. Instead you were concentrating very hard on what X was saying in order to follow how the lecture was constructed and the reasoning, explanations, examples, etc. that were being given, possibly only noting down a few words or phrases that you thought were important and would help you to reconstruct the content later. Your notepaper was yellow and you were writing using a mixture of capital letters for what you considered to be key terms and non-capitals for supporting information.

All of these associated details make the context of that particular lecture more vivid. Any one of the details you deliberately tried to fix in your mind can jog your memory of the event. You can access content details by ascertain visualising, for example, the words you wrote in capital letters and

R   how they stood out on the yellow paper. The more access routes you reinforce provide into a context the more readily you can recall it.

Primacy and Recency Effects

You will probably be familiar with some kind of memory game you played as a child or have seen on television which involves trying to remember as many different objects as possible having only seen them once. Kim's game, named after a character from a Rudyard Kipling novel, who was training to become a spy, is one such game. Similar procedures have been conducted in psychological research on memory, and it has been found that people usually remember what they saw first and what they saw last and things that were particularly striking. Remembering what you saw or heard first is known as the *primacy effect*, and remembering what you saw or heard last is referred to as the *recency* effect.

You can use these effects to make a memory game out of a topic that you are studying. For example, try to remember the main words in the first three sentences you read in a section or hear in a lecture, and do the same for the last three sentences you read. In a lecture, you're unlikely to know exactly when the lecture is going to end, but think back on the ending immediately afterwards and try to remember the actual words the lecturer used.

You can also try to apply primacy and recency effects to the reader of your own essays. This means making sure your introductory paragraph is clear and focused, showing that you have understood the import of the title, and signalling for the reader how your argument is likely to develop. This gives the primacy effect. Even if the essay goes a bit awry at some points, the reader is likely to remember a strong beginning. The situation is similar for the ending. The effect of what you have read last can be more enduring. Therefore working on getting final paragraphs to act as summaries of your argument without repeating everything you have said is also a very good idea.

BEING SYSTEMATIC

In the ancient Greek system of 'places', things that you had to remember were stored in an orderly fashion so that they could be retrieved more easily. By remembering the order of places so thoroughly that you could 'find your way' both forward and backwards, you were assured of always 'finding' what it was you had to remember.

Similarly, libraries store books according to a particular classification system, such as the Dewey decimal system (see Table 4.1 in Chapter 4), which means that books on a particular subject such as philosophy, psychology, sociology, or education are stored together.

The crucial point is that whatever mnemonic techniques you use, or however you choose to organise your material, you must be systematic.

^{ascertain} **C** A simple, if somewhat gruesome, illustration of a system helping recall comes from the ancient Greek legend associated with the alleged inventor of systems for helping the memory, Simonides. He was the only one to survive a disaster, having been called away from a banquet just before the building it was being held in collapsed. All the other participants at the banquet were killed and their bodies so destroyed as to be unrecognisable. Simonides was able to identify them by remembering their positions at the table and relating where each mangled body lay to that position. It basically doesn't matter what your system is and it may be different for different topics of study, although there are definite advantages in maintaining a reusable system such as keeping your own conventions in terms of colour, capital letters, bullet points, and so on, for classifying things in order of importance or analytical difference.

classify

System and Short-Term Memory

The cognitive psychologist George Miller (1956) found out that our capacity for remembering things and keeping them within our short-term or working memory revolved around the number 7. The memorable phrase he coined to relate this was *seven plus or minus two*. This means that the maximum number of things you are likely to be able to keep in your mind at any one time is nine. Seven is the average number of things that people are likely to be working with, and five is a comfortable number. It is interesting that the ancient orators were trained to remember things in groups of five. At every fifth place in the architectural system a golden hand, for example, would be placed alongside the anchor or weapon that was otherwise there. This might mean, for example, that they had to remember five groups of five places, rather than 25 places. Grouping helps you to remember more by actually reducing the amount that you have to remember.

For example, you can count up the number of elements related to any topic that you want to remember. The process of deciding on which elements to remember is also useful as it in itself involves analysing or breaking the topic down in some way. Ideally, the things that you want to remember – ideas, names of people and places, dates, the points for and against an argument – should be words that act like containers. This means that when you remember them, they spark off more associations. The 'game' is to remember both the amount of things that you have isolated, and what they are. If you limit yourself to nine things in accordance with the seven plus or minus two formula, and group them in threes, go over them in your mind a few times initially, and then try and recall them at odd moments, say when you're standing in a bus queue or while you're in the bath, you stand a good chance of remembering them. Figure 2.2 shows an example of grouping related to this chapter.

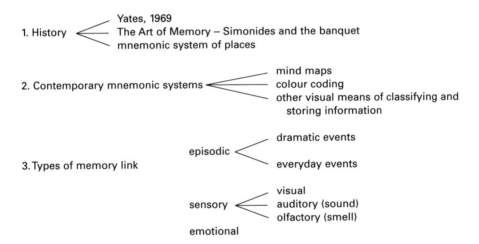

Figure 2.2   *Remembering about memory*

RISKING MISTAKES

Making mistakes can also be memorable and can therefore also be a good learning experience. In Chapter 9 I talk about the benefits of trying out words or constructions which are new to you. This is a risk-taking strategy because you risk getting things wrong. However, the fact that your tutor has to correct you, along with the fact that you were perhaps aware of your uncertainty in the first place, ultimately reinforces what is right.

Attempting to override any anxieties you may have concerning the study context can be risk-taking. For example, listening to a lecture and not taking any notes can be a risk-taking strategy if you are not very confident about understanding the lecture. However, it might also be something you need to do in order to boost your confidence about understanding lectures as you listen to them. There is a particular benefit to not taking notes. By not having to focus on writing things down, you have more available resources for concentrating on understanding. This also gives you an opportunity to put a memorable recording and retrieval system into action!

FURTHER PRACTICE

A range of different examples and simple exercises on mnemonic techniques can be found in Buzan's (1986) book, *Use Your Memory*, if you would like further practice.

SUMMARY

Your memory can be actively involved in learning. This means thinking constructively about *how* you are storing what you are learning in your mind. This both helps the learning process and makes it easier to *recall* what you've learned.

Learning and aiding recall are intertwined. Both can be helped by the deliberate application of strategies for storage and retrieval. The strategies include *mnemonic techniques*. Mnemonics can be visual or verbal or a combination of both, and allow you to use your imagination. Different aspects of memory can all be activated in making things stand out. The more vivid, lurid, or grotesque your mnemonics are, the more easily you will remember them and the associations that go with them.

The process of setting up any storage system in your memory needs to be systematic. Thinking out your system is also helping you to organise your learning. Your system should be orderly and consistent, and ideally reusable. It is important, however, *to stick to it!*

two

31

3

Managing your Time

warm-up exercise
Which of the following can you hear yourself saying?

- ➤ I can only work when I've got a deadline
- ➤ I make sure I read something connected to my studies every day
- ➤ I need to work and re-work things until I'm really satisfied with it
- ➤ It takes me ages to read a book

Discussion

The above comments all have some relationship to the use of study time and the effectiveness of time-related strategies to managing your studies. Some people do work better when they have got a definite deadline. They may not have the self-discipline to get down to some serious work otherwise, or it may be the case that there are too many different activities or assignments competing for their time. To restrict yourself only to this strategy, however, is likely to lead to trouble. Deadlines for different assignments might be near each other, for example, and you don't have enough quality time to turn around from thinking about one subject to thinking about the next.

The second and third comments sound more like good common sense in the study context. However, there is a difference between reading something related to your studies every day because it makes you feel good, and reading purposefully. An example of purposeful reading would be to read about a particular topic in different textbooks, say a chapter from each, in order to prepare yourself for an essay on that topic. Working and reworking your writing conforms well to good writing practice. You need time to draft and redraft your work. However, it's also important not to get too anxious about perfection. There's no such thing as the perfect essay. You should do your best, but you should also remember that you can learn from feedback. It's therefore better to make sure you get your work handed in on time so that you can benefit from your tutor's comments and be in a position to improve your essay writing technique next time around.

The comment about taking ages to read a book sounds like it comes from someone who is not aware of different reading strategies and just ploughs straight ahead. If you heard yourself agreeing with that comment, then you can start to look at some of the reading strategies discussed in Chapter 6.

THINKING ABOUT TIME

TASK 3.1

Think of at least five expressions that we use with the word 'time'. For example, can we 'put on' time? No, but we can …

1   .... time

2   .... time

3   .... time

4   .... time

5   .... time

Discussion

The verbs that we use with the word 'time' such as *save, spend, waste*, give an insight into how we conceptualise or think about time. (Throughout this chapter, words that work as metaphors for thinking about time will be written in italics. However, these words by no means cover all the possibilities.)

Thinking about how we routinely talk about such things as time makes us more aware of its place in our culture. The verbs *save, spend,* and *waste* are in fact *metaphors.* They show that we tend to think of time in the same way as we think of money. This link points up the fact that time is something that is valued in our culture. It is a rather precious commodity which we prefer to *spend* carefully rather than *waste.*

The notion of *saving* time is linked with speed, which in the economic context is linked with efficiency, and brings together the importance of time and money. The expression *time is money* is often used. Time is also very much caught up in the *economy* of managing your studies. It is not so much a question of always doing things quickly however, as *getting the timing right.* In the study context, *time is learning!*

TIME AND STUDY STRATEGIES

Most of us complain about there not being enough time for us to do all that we want to do. This is likely to apply also to your studies. *Estimating* the time it takes to do something and avoiding *running out of* time are two major study skills.

TASK 3.2

Here are a few common study tasks. How long do you think on average it would take you to do them?

Study tasks	Time taken
1 Read a book with 10 chapters	
2 Read one chapter in a book, say 12–15 pages	
3 Take notes from one chapter	
4 Clear a space on your desk so that you can work comfortably	
5 Sharpen your pencils, get paper together, find a bookmark for your book, make sure you have a rubber handy	

6	Brainstorm	
7	Write the first draft of an essay	
8	Get started writing for an essay	
9	Read through your notes before starting to write an essay	
10	Surf the net	

Discussion

The above tasks obviously vary in terms of the length of time you are likely to spend on them. However, that in itself gives a perspective on time and how it relates to managing your studies. You may accomplish a great deal in a very short time, for example, if you manage to have a very effective brainstorming session where you very quickly get down on paper all the different aspects of a topic that you want to include in an essay. On the other hand, something can drag on for a long time and not actually result in very much. You might spend ages reading every word of a book but not really have much of a sense of what it is all about by the end of it. The latter is an example of not using your time effectively. Time management should be a constructive element in effective learning.

Saving Time or Wasting Time

In reading through the above tasks, it probably occurred to you that some of them might be a question of time wasting rather than time-saving. It is a good idea for example to clear a space on your desk before you begin working, on the principle that a clear space aids clear thinking. It is also a good idea to have everything to hand that you might need in the course of a study session. However, tidying up your desk or sharpening your pencils are also the kinds of things that students famously (or perhaps infamously) do *instead of* getting down to work. Set yourself a limit for such things. Three minutes for example, is all you need to file some things away that are lying on your desk, find the books you want, your notebook and pen or pencil, and sit down!

How the management of time and task is best accomplished might not always be obvious, however. Two different tasks which might at first glance seem to be longer and shorter versions of the same thing, such as tasks 1 and 2, reading a whole book and reading a chapter of a book, might be most effectively done if the same amount of time is *allotted* to each. It is a question of reading strategies and of *prioritising* where you are most likely to get the answers you are looking for (see Chapter 6 on reading strategies).

A task such as 3, taking notes from your reading, may take more or less time depending on your note-taking strategy. You may be concentrating on making your notes memorable, as discussed in the previous chapter, and this might require careful work which takes up more time. This could be time well spent if your note-taking system is clearly thought out and implemented. Here time, study strategy, and effective learning are integrated. Note-making from your reading may be something that is worth *investing* time in.

On the other hand, if you resort to the simple strategy of copying down sentences exactly as they are written in the book, this is more likely to be time wasting. Time is better spent actually thinking about what you are reading, processing the information as it were, asking yourself questions about it and how it relates to other aspects of the subject. The note taking stage will come afterwards, when you reflect on what you've read and put down notes in your own words. As well as engaging more deeply with the topic, you will also be avoiding any risk of inadvertent plagiarism (see also _{ascertain} the comments on plagiarism in Chapter 9). *Putting in* time and effort

R is always likely to be more productive than something which is time-
_{reflect} consuming but doesn't really work your brain.

Net Time

The area of technology is an interesting one in relation to time, as it is not always time saving. Easy access to information via the internet can *cut out* lots of time searching for it for example, but using the internet is possibly also one of the biggest sources of time wasting available to students. You can waste a lot of time looking at 'joke' sites or sites that are otherwise amusing or interesting but not particularly useful. 'Web' sites are aptly named. You can be drawn into one like insects into a spider's web. They are often deliberately made attractive to lure you in.

You need to be fairly focused and carefully target the hypertext keys that are most likely to give you access to the information you want. You need therefore to narrow down the question you are asking. Putting in a search for a topic that is very general is likely to throw up hundreds, if not thousands of possibilities and you risk 'drowning' rather than 'surfing'. As a general rule, if you haven't found something genuinely useful to you after a search of 10 minutes, give it up.

Pacing Yourself

Pacing yourself is another way of maximising your efforts to learn. It is difficult to take in a lot at any one time, especially when things are new to you. Spreading your learning over a period of time can help you to remember things. It enables reinforcement of the data, which makes it more memorable, and therefore more likely to become information that you have easily at your disposal, should you need to refer to it. You may even lodge such information so well in your memory that you can use it long after you complete the actual assignment relating to it.

The drafting and re-drafting of essays is an example of pacing yourself. Writing a first draft can be a speedy process or something that you work long and hard on. However, the element of timing that it highlights is not so much the time the first draft in itself takes but how far *in advance of* the deadline you are doing it. You need to work back from the deadline and *allow* time for the different stages of getting an essay to the handing in stage.

In the case of reading, the strategies of first reading the first sentence in each paragraph and then reading the whole chapter also enact a pacing procedure. The two different paces of reading complement each other. In combination, they are more effective in reinforcing the content of the reading than simply reading through the chapter (see Chapter 6 on reading).

Testing yourself on what you have learnt after the elapse of some time is another pacing procedure. It is one which conforms to the principle of reinforcement in learning, talked about also in Chapter 4. The reinforcement principle works as follows:

> ➤ test your existing knowledge
> ➤ identify any gaps
> ➤ go back to your sources
> ➤ clarify your knowledge

More on the importance of pacing will be said in Chapter 8 on the management of examinations. Here, the trick is to avoid what might be thought of as the opposite of pacing, namely cramming.

Cramming may be effective in the short term, but it is likely that there will just simply be too much to remember. Cramming for exams may be seen as a 'leaving things until the last minute' strategy. In other words, it has negative associations with time.

PLANNING WHEN TO DO YOUR STUDIES

TASK 3.3

Look at the following timetable for a week with the hours from 8.00am - 2.00am marked off. Can you think about your current week or next week and plot out as clearly as possible when you think you will be studying and when you will be doing other things?

Discussion

In the exercise of going through how you spend your time you'll probably have idealised the amount of time spent doing certain things. If you put down 2 hours studying for example, not all of that time will have been spent in productive studying. However, you could also argue that the minuscule (of course!) amounts of time that weren't spent in that way were helping the productive time by giving your mind a break.

It is also likely that you did not put down the time you spent 'faffing around' as a contemporary idiom would put it. In order to plan your study time well, you need to build in non-study time. You also need to differentiate between different kinds of time, such as *quality time* where you get down to some serious work and 'faffing' time where you take time off as it were from being purposeful about what you do with your time.

	Monday	Tuesday	Wednesday	Thursday	Friday	Saturday	Sunday
8.00							
9.00							
10.00							
11.00							
12.00							
13.00							
14.00							
15.00							
16.00							

17.00	18.00	19.00	20.00	21.00	22.00	23.00	24.00	1.00	2.00	

Prioritising Task and Time

You need to be able to *prioritise* what you have to do. This means giving a value to the different things that have to be done and arranging them in order of importance. This may not necessarily mean however that you do what you think is the most important thing first. You need to think also in terms of *quality* time. Some study tasks or study sessions will require better quality time than others. Quality time can be at any time of day, but one where you are unlikely to have too many things clogging up your mind, and when you're not in a hurry to go off somewhere else. It is also important that you feel alert, so perhaps first thing in the morning or late afternoon, or even midnight on occasion if that suits (see below)!

There is a limit to how long you can spend in rapt concentration. So it's a good idea to plan breaks in your quality time. The average amount of time you can spend concentrating on something is about 20 minutes, but this is a bit too short for every study session. However, a forty-minute slot, allowing for a break of a minute or so to straighten your shoulders, or look out the window, can be quite productive.

TASK 3.4

Write a prioritisation check-list. List up to five things that you have to do (it can be a mixture of study-related and other things) and think of the best time for you to do each in the course of two days.

Discussion

Quality study time need not mean blocking off long stretches of time. You can plan your study time around or alongside other things that you have to do or want to do. If for instance, there's a TV programme you want to watch, try and fit in a 40-minute study slot at either side of it. That way, you've got something to look forward to and also something memorable between the two slots. You could use this pattern to help you remember what you were studying during the two sessions. Similarly, you could plan to do a couple of hours studying before you get ready to go to a party. This strategy of rewarding yourself for time spent studying can be very effective. Thinking of particular times as boundaries around study periods can also force you to get more done than if you plan to keep a whole day free. The sense of lots of time can lull you into a false sense of productivity.

Maximising your study time without blanking out whole chunks of time can be achieved in other ways as well. Not everything you put in the hour slots in the timetable above, for example, will have necessarily taken a full hour. Think about how you might have productively used the extra minutes. You might have allowed yourself an hour for lunch but it doesn't have to take up that much time. Perhaps you could have nipped into the library for fifteen minutes either before or after to get that book you wanted to take out. You might have to take a bus or train between where you live and the university. You can use that time to skim read or survey read if the conditions aren't quite right for more concentrated reading. The point is that it does pay to *think ahead* and work out when you might be able to do something rather than just blithely hope that everything will get done.

ascertain A anticipate

Burning the Midnight Oil

Burning the midnight oil is almost a necessary ritual of student life, although it won't suit all students, particularly those who have families. Its usual association is with essay deadlines and with preparing for exams. An essay has to be handed in the next day and in a desperate attempt to get it done, a student stays up all night. There is nothing wrong with staying up all night. There may be fewer distractions, allowing you to work in peace. The problem arises when there is no time for editing and re-drafting and the first fruit of your labours is what gets handed in. One all-night splurge may beat the deadline but not show your writing at its best. Continued burning of the midnight oil, whether in study or otherwise (!), is bound to interfere with your studies. Avoiding or being half asleep for nine o'clock lectures, for example, will not help you get to grips with your studies.

Getting to the Degree Stage

Planning your time and managing your studies also applies to the larger framework of getting a degree, which will normally take three or four years. The first year is usually a foundation year and somewhat easier going than the others. However, this should not be an excuse to give this year less attention. The foundation year is like the foundation of a building, it is what you build on later. It gives you time to work out the system (every university is a bit different), to get some idea of the scope of the subject you are studying, or the range of modules if it is a modular degree, and a chance to become familiar with the conventions of academic writing, among other things.

The rather strange term 'exit velocity' may be used in some institutions for the idea that marks gained in your final year are worth more than those gained in your first or second years. This does not, however, mean that your first year doesn't count at all. If you don't make a start on your reading or getting to grips with complex ideas or concepts in this year, it is very difficult to catch up in later years, since the workload will definitely increase in those years. So enjoy the lighter load but don't waste your time, or treat the year as if it didn't matter.

SUMMARY

The main message of this chapter has been that good time management and effective learning go hand in hand. The major time management strategies can be thought of as *the three p's*. They are:

➢ Planning ahead
➢ Pacing yourself
➢ Prioritisation

Consciously increase your awareness of time and the amount of time different things take, in order to improve your planning.

Part Two
ACADEMIC TASKS AND CONTEXTS

The emphasis in this part of the book is on you actively taking control of the tasks you are set in the academic context. You therefore need to understand why you are asked to do them, what the criteria are for a good written assignment or seminar presentation for example, and be able to put into practice the kinds of strategies that are most effective in getting you the results you want.

The section is divided into five chapters. Chapter 4 looks at strategies for managing your assignments and general principles of good practice as a student – for example, how you use the library and how you structure the process of crafting a good written assignment.

Chapter 5 focuses on the essay. You are taken behind the scenes to look more closely at the criteria behind how your essays are assessed and given some strategies as to how to proceed and what to be aware of.

Chapter 6 looks at reading strategies and how to use them to match the purpose of your reading as well as to get through the amount of reading you have to do.

Chapter 7 looks at the purpose of seminars and the process of giving seminar presentations.

Chapter 8 looks at approaches to the examination process and strategies for managing revision.

The overall aims of Part Two are:

➢ to give you strategies that you might use to help you improve your approach to learning;
➢ to help you evaluate the different kinds of attitude and strategies that are available and encourage you to find out what works best for you;
➢ to help you to become an independent and therefore lifelong learner.

4

Managing your Assignments

warm-up exercise
How do you approach your studies?

1   Do you subscribe to the so-called jungle book method, that is 'doing the bare necessities'?
2   Do you spend your time between the coffee shop and the bar, only occasionally attending a lecture or seminar?
3   Do you rigorously do everything you're asked to do and also follow up ideas you're particularly interested in?
4   Do you basically saunter along, lying in when you feel like it and occasionally staying up all night to write an essay?

Discussion

The above descriptions are essentially stereotypes. It is unlikely that any student actually fits any of them entirely, although most students will probably be able to identify with some of them at least some of the time during their studies. While some of them may appear to be negative stereotypes of student life, even those descriptions implicitly contain strategies that can be positive on occasion. Similarly, what seems to be a positive strategy, namely trying to cover everything thoroughly, may be counter-productive: you have to prioritise, and give more time and effort to those assignments that count most towards your degree or those areas you have most difficulty getting to grips with.

The 'bare necessities' approach is an extreme example of strategic thinking, i.e. thinking only of the degree at the end and not thinking too much about the quality of the learning that goes on in the middle.

ascertain
S
select

It is not to be recommended, but it does make sense to make sure you know how the assessment system works for your degree.

Having 'fun' at university is an important part of university life, but a balance has to be struck. You can make the 'fun' parts a reward for hard work. So for example, you can plan a visit to the coffee shop or bar *after* you have done some reading or writing. This is also a useful time management strategy, as discussed in Chapter 3.

ASSIGNMENT TYPES

TASK 4.1

Here is a list of different types of university assignment: reports, essays, presentations, share portfolios, lab reports, surveys, learning journal, progress diary, summaries, multiple-choice exercises, short paragraph answers to a number of different questions on the same topic, mini research projects.

1 Which of them apply to you?
2 Which do you consider the most difficult?
3 Why?

Submitting course work is an essential part of any degree programme. However, it takes different forms on different courses and each type of course work places different demands on you, as you will be aware if you have answered questions 2 and 3 above.

As the number of different types of assignment is growing you are likely to have to cope with several different kinds. This means that you have to use language in different ways, it means that you may have to learn to work in groups as well as on your own, it also means that as you are doing a particular assignment you learn skills which you can use in other situations as well. Experience of working in a group, of delegating and being delegated to, of knowing that the group relies on your contribution can be of use when it comes to looking for a job after university. These abilities are known as 'transferable' skills and are an important part of a university education.

ascertain

transfer
skills

four

48

PLANNING AND PREPARATION

There are a number of things which you need to think of before you begin an assignment. They include:

➢ consulting departmental guidelines;
➢ assessing the purpose of the assignment;
➢ working out how much it counts;
➢ constructing a bibliography.

Consulting Departmental Guidelines

Every student receives a handbook, containing a great deal of information about your programme of study. Many students do not read it in detail, at least not at first, when they are given it at the beginning of their courses. However, it is extremely important that you hang on to it for reference, as there will be times when you need the guidance it gives. Not all tutors are pleased to have to spend time telling you about things which they know are in the handbook and which therefore you can get access to yourself.

Such student handbooks contain guidelines on written assignments, including the preferred conventions for bibliographies. However, an example of the two most common systems is given below.

Purpose

Each type of assignment will have been set for different purposes, and it makes sense for you to think about what that purpose is before you begin. This has implications for how you should best tackle an assignment. For example, the task may have been set to test your ability to undertake some practical research, put the findings in statistical form, and then assess the outcome. You will need to address all three of those purposes.

Assessment Weighting

One purpose that all assignments serve is assessment. However, the weighting of each assessment is different. Some count towards your overall mark for the year and some don't. Those that count are likely also to be differently weighted – one may be worth 20% and another 40%. You need to bear those issues in mind when you're prioritising your workload, although this does not mean that you ignore the 'less important' assignment. At one level, all assignments are important in that they offer you an opportunity to test your knowledge and/or to practise skills, such as writing up lab reports or writing essays, which you need to acquire.

Constructing a Bibliography

It is important that you keep a meticulous record of every book you read relating to your course. This record should include the following information:

➢ the full name of the author;
➢ the title of the book;
➢ the date of publication;
➢ the place of publication;
➢ the name of the publisher.

When you write an essay, you will often need to list at the end of it all the books and articles you have referred to in the text. There are a number of ways of doing this. Both Sage, the publishers of this book, and the American Psychological Association (APA), for example, use similar variations on the Harvard or author–date system for writing up bibliographies. These begin by recording the author's (or authors') surname(s), followed by the year of publication.

Next comes the title of the work being cited. At this point, there is a difference between whether you're citing a book, a chapter in a book, or an article in a journal. For a book, you need to record its title, the place of publication and the name of the publisher. Some systems may put the place of publication last.

For a chapter in a book, the title of the chapter is followed by the word 'in' and the title of the book, the name(s) of the book's editor(s), the place of publication, the name of publisher and the page numbers of the chapter. The order these come in depends on the system used.

For an article in a journal, the sequence after the title of the article is: the name of journal, the volume number and (where necessary) issue number of journal, and the page numbers of the article.

Here are three references in the APA system for a book, a chapter in an edited book, and a journal article:

Cameron, D. (1995) *Verbal Hygiene*. London: Routledge.
Lillis, T. (1999). Whose 'common sense'? Essayist literacy and the institutional practice of mystery. In C. Jones, J. Turner, & B. Street (Eds.), *Students writing in the university: cultural and epistemological issues* (pp. 127–147). Amsterdam: John Benjamins.
Bartholomae, D. (1986). Inventing the university. *Journal of Basic Writing,* 5(1), 4–22.

Compare these with Sage's style for references at the back of this book. For further details of the APA style for references, see APA (1994).

The citation for an internet document should follow a format similar to that for print, with some imformation omitted and some added. Here is an example of how to cite a document posted on APA's own website:

Jacobson, J.W., Mulick, J.A., & Schwartz, A.A. (1995). A history of facilitated communication: Science, pseudoscience, and antiscience: Science working group on facilitated communication. *American Psychologist, 50,* 750–765. Retrieved January 25, 1996, from the World Wide Web: http://www.apa.org/journals/ jacobson.html

The reference begins with the same information that would be provided for a printed source. The internet address is then placed in a retrieval statement, with the date on which the material was accessed, at the end of the reference. This is important as documents on the internet may change in content, move, or be removed from a site altogether.

FOLLOWING UP FEEDBACK

It is customary on most university courses to give back assignments along with a feedback sheet outlining the main criteria for assessment (see examples in Chapter 5) and commenting on each area. These feedback sheets offer a crucial opportunity for you to focus on the areas which have been highlighted as having room for improvement.

There is a tendency for students to refer only to their mark and not to take much notice of comments. If you do this, you are wasting the chance of improving your skills in completing that particular type of assignment.

Feedback does not just come through separate feedback sheets, your lecturer may also make comments in the margin or comments at the end of what you've written.

Ivanič et al. (2000: 55) have identified the following six categories for the different kinds of feedback comments that you get from your reader/assessor. These are:

> ➢ explain [your] grade in terms of strengths and weaknesses;
> ➢ correct or edit [your] work;
> ➢ evaluate the match between [your] essay and an 'ideal' answer;
> ➢ engage in dialogue with [you]; for example they say things like: 'that's an interesting idea' or 'why are you telling me this here?'
> ➢ give advice which will be useful in writing the next essay;
> ➢ give advice on rewriting the essay.

It is important that you understand any comments that your tutor makes. If your tutor's handwriting is difficult to read for example (spare a thought for the number of texts they have to respond to), you should make a point of going to see him or her and getting clarification. This applies also if a comment is made which you don't quite understand.

Ask if you're not sure!

YOUR USE OF THE LIBRARY

How you use the library is an important part of managing the study process as a whole. You should become familiar with the cataloguing system and how to access it. You are most likely to do this via the

Table 4.1 *Dewey Decimal Classification System*	
000–099	General Reference
100–199	Philosophy and Psychology
200–299	Religion
300–399	Social Sciences
400–499	Languages
500–599	Science
600–699	Technology & Applied Science
700–799	Fine Art & Music
800–899	Literature
900–999	Geography & History

computer terminals in your library. Most universities provide inductions into accessing their information systems, which you should make sure you attend. Table 4.1 shows a breakdown of the Dewey decimal classification system, which is how most libraries catalogue their books. Make sure that you are familiar with this system, so that you know where to look for books on your subject(s). Sometimes it is helpful even just to browse around the relevant shelves. You get an awareness of the range of what's been written about your subject area and you might find something of interest.

Thinking Ahead

One of the most important study strategies associated with using the library is to think ahead. For example, no library these days can afford to have enough books for every student to be able to take out what they want when they want it. Once an assignment has been set, there is likely to be a high demand for those books that are on the reading list for it. You therefore have to get to the library as quickly as possible in order to get at least one of the books out that you need. Do not wait until after the coffee break – go immediately to the library!

Often reading lists are given out at the start of term, and it would do no harm to have taken some books out even *before* you have been specifically pointed towards them, to get an overview of what they are about. When an assignment does come in, you will know immediately whether the particular book(s) you have out has some relevance to the topic, and be able to read it more carefully immediately. What this also means of course is that you are likely to be the one being asked to 'return the book requested by another reader'!

The amount of time you are allowed to take books out for usually varies between 3 and 4 weeks for a regular loan. If there is no demand from other students, you can renew the book for a further loan period if you need to.

Most departments have a 'short loan' system which means that books can only be taken out for one week, three days, or sometimes even overnight. This system is in fairness to all those who would like to have access to the books. In the case of books that are in high demand, there is likely to be a 'reference only' copy in the library. This means you can only look at the book in the library, but at least you know you can have a look at it!

The fact that you may only be able to get hold of books for a limited period of time means that you should take reading strategies seriously (see Chapter 6). Developing good reading habits will help you to get as much as possible from the books before you have to hand them back. You cannot possibly photocopy everything – and anyway photocopying is a delaying tactic, putting off actual learning for another time.

Read and take notes rather than only photocopy!

Working Together

Another way round not being able to get hold of books you need immediately is to work with a friend or – even better – a group of friends. You can then share the book that one of you has got out. You might even be able to divide up the relevant sections in the book between or among you. It is actually a good learning strategy to have to tell somebody else what you have read about in a way that makes it clear to them.

MAKING THE MOST OF MAKING NOTES

Managing your assignments, of whatever type, will usually involve you in making notes. Making notes seems a particularly simple activity, but in fact it is quite complex and worthy of some thought. Here are some questions to get you going. Compare and discuss your responses with others.

TASK 4.2

Question	Yes	No
1 Do you meticulously copy out whole chunks of text from books or from other people's notes?		
2 Do you read a section or chapter of a book first and then try to make your own summary?		
3 Do you write down a few sentences that might be suitable for quoting?		
4 If you write down what might make a good quote, do you always record the page on which it is found, as well as the title, date of publication and author of the book?		
5 Do you read a section or chapter of a book first and then make a mind-map of what you have read?		
6 Do you always take notes from lectures?		
7 Do you try to write down as much as possible of what the lecturer says?		
8 Do you start in the middle of an A4 page and draw a mind map of the issues the lecturer touches on as s/he goes through the lecture?		
9 Do you feel that you've done more work, the more notes you've written?		
10 Do you see note making as an opportunity to be creative or colourful?		

four

55

Discussion

What are the issues to do with taking and making notes? From observing and listening to what students say about this, there are at least the following issues:

> ➢ Feeling more or less secure about what information you've got.
> ➢ Having a conflict of focus, for example listening or writing – but not both.
> ➢ Feeling more or less confident about your ability to remember.
> ➢ Feeling that you should be using a particular method, for example brainstorming and drawing a tree diagram, but not feeling comfortable with that.
> ➢ Not really giving it any thought at all.
>
> From these points, it is clear that making notes is tied up with psychological issues of fear, uncertainty and lack of confidence. These larger psychological issues are of course not only felt in regard to note-taking, but we can see note-taking as a microcosm of how these factors are involved in – some would argue get in the way of – the learning process itself.

Copying Down or Integrating into your Thinking?

Given the above discussion of anxiety about getting things right, it is hardly surprising that a lot of students spend ages meticulously taking down notes in the exact wording of the text, whether in a book or on an acetate projected by the lecturer during a lecture. This gives a sense of security that when you return to your notes for revision purposes or for writing an assignment, the information you have will be accurate and reliable.

However, what you might be neglecting by doing this all the time is the opportunity to actually process what's going on in the text as you're reading it or reading and listening to the lecturer at the same time. If you are fully alert and trying to follow the argument or description, the chances are you will retain ascertain more by the end than if you are concentrating on copying everything E down exactly. Copying is a relatively simple activity, and in doing it you engage are unlikely to fully engage your brain with the subject matter.

Copying down the exact wording from textbooks can also be a dangerous activity. When you come back to your notes as a whole it may not always be clear what you have formulated and what has come from the textbook. If you do not put exact wordings in quotes, you are open to the accusation of plagiarism, an offence which is taken very seriously. The issue of plagiarism is developed further in Chapter 9.

I do not want to suggest that you should never copy something down exactly, just that you should be discriminating about it and also be prepared to *take risks* with your own sense of your ability to understand and remember things. In cases where exact definitions are required, for example, perhaps in law-related subjects or where any technical terms need to be clearly defined, then copying down exactly the first time, and perhaps several times again from memory, is a good idea.

If you lack confidence in yourself as a learner – and most people do at some stage, particularly in areas new to them – you have to take risks with yourself in order to prove to yourself that you can do it. The beginning of your studies is a good time to do this as you can afford the risk of getting things wrong. Therefore try to make notes **after** reading or listening. In the case of reading, you can always go back to the text to make sure (see procedures for managing the essay-writing process, below). You cannot go back to a lecture, as it were, but you can consult other students who were at the lecture and even the lecturer her/himself after the next lecture, for example. In addition, there is always likely to be a reading list for back-up.

ascertain

R

risk

four

57

Your first attempt at this strategy may not be brilliant, but as you become more familiar with the material and the kind of organising signals in texts that highlight what is important (see, for example, the section on reading the first sentences of paragraphs in Chapter 6) you should improve.

Disciplining Yourself to Make Notes from Recall

It takes a great deal of self-discipline to make sure you actually make notes after a lecture or after a period of reading. However, even if you only spend 5 minutes after a lecture writing down what immediately struck you as most important, the fact of actually writing something down and forcing yourself to think back on what you've just heard will itself act as a trigger to remembering other things later on.

You might also find yourself wanting to add things later on in the day. For this reason, it's always good to have some Post-It notes with you. They are more easily carried than A4 notebooks, so you have no excuse!

Notes do not simply serve a recording function, they function best when you are learning by writing them.

Note-making Processes

The traditional way of making notes is to write in short phrases and arrange them under sub-headings in vertical sequence on the page. This is known as *linear* note-making. Linear note-making is associated with left brain functions, emphasising the traditional academic skills of verbal reasoning and organising. Right brain functions, on the other hand, are concerned with visual and spatial ability as well as creativity. Note-making is an area where those right brain functions can be put to good use, especially if you have a strong visual awareness and like to organise things in a visual manner. Mind maps, as discussed in Chapter 2 in relation to memory, are a good example of a visual-spatial approach to arranging notes. There are, however, a number of different ways in which the information you record can be visually and spatially arranged, both to make the recording process easier and what is recorded more memorable.

dividing the page

Dividing an A4 page down the middle cuts the amount of expanse in half and enables you to classify information according to which half of the page you are putting it on. It might be for example that you put names or ideas on one side and illustrative examples or other supporting material on the other side. You can use this procedure during lectures or when taking notes from your reading. It tends to leave you more space to play with afterwards, so you can add things or group things together to show their relationships more clearly.

the spider diagram

This refers to a diagram for recording information that looks a bit like a spider. In taking notes from a lecture, for example, rather than start at the top of the page, you begin in the middle with the main topic and draw out tentacles and sub-tentacles from it, as the lecturer develops the topic. This enables you to get an idea of the number of different facets that belong to the topic in a memorable visual image. If the lecturer takes the topic in one direction in particular, your spider may be a little lop-sided, but that doesn't matter. It shows clearly where the emphasis within the topic has been. By noting how some of the 'tentacles' are further developed at a later stage, you gain a closer understanding of the 'shape' of the topic as a whole.

Maintaining a Filing System

Of course, there is no point in putting a lot of effort into making notes if you don't file them adequately. You need to have a filing system. Perhaps the simplest filing system is to have an A4 ring binder for each of your courses. You can then put lecture notes, handouts, and notes from your own reading into the binder. It is worth taking time at the end of every day to make sure you put your notes into the relevant binder. For example, if you write Post-It note add-ons to the notes you tried writing from recall, you'll have to add your Post-It notes to the original, carefully dated sheet of paper (likely to be A4, and possibly already safely housed in your folder for that course) as soon as possible, rather than run the risk of losing them.

In anticipation of an easily accessible filing system, you should:

➤ Always date your work.
➤ Always record your sources, for example lecture on X by Y, or the exact details of the book you're reading as noted above on the section on constructing a bibliography.
➤ Keep your notes for different courses separate. For example, don't write notes from the second lecture you attend on the back of the A4 sheet you finished on for the first lecture.
➤ Keep a ready supply of A4, holed paper, for ease of filing and consistency of size.

If you have a more specialised filing system going, such as different ascertain coloured paper for different courses, and different coloured inks for **C** highlighting different kinds of content, then you must make sure that classify you always have a ready supply of paper and pens with you.

Keeping a good filing system is part of being generally well organised, or at least being student-like. For example, the student who turns up at a seminar and needs to borrow a pen and paper is not being at all student-like. You don't need to carry your ring binders around with you, but you should at least have the basics with you at all times.

INTEGRATING WRITING, READING AND NOTE-MAKING IN MANAGING WRITTEN ASSIGNMENTS

Written assignments such as essays take time both to research and to write, and you need to build this time into the process. A suitable time-span might be three or four weeks. While the ultimate product is a piece of written work, the process of getting there includes taking notes and reading in an efficient and effective way (see also Chapter 6).

Here is a possible step-by-step procedure for managing a written assignment.

1   Read your title carefully, as this will give you the orientation for your argumentation, report, account or whatever.
2   Underline the key structure words in the title (words like discuss, to what extent, what, how, describe, give an account).
3   Write as much as you can based on simply thinking through what the title demands and putting down what you know or remember from lectures, previous reading, etc.
4   From the above brainstorming-type exercise, you will inevitably reach blocks – you can't think of an example, you don't know exactly why X is the case, you can't remember the details exactly – so …
5   Go back to your reading – look specifically for back-up on the points you couldn't go any further with. This is where you 'scan' the text, looking only for specific information. See Chapter 6 for further discussion.
6   Do further background reading on the subject and take relevant notes. For example, ask questions such as 'What does X say on the subject?'.
7   Try to take your notes after your reading rather than during – that way you are more likely to use your own wording, and it's also a good test of whether you've understood. (It's also a good way of avoiding plagiarism: see Chapter 9.)
8   If you find you get stuck on what exactly the point, argument or definition was, go back again to the text.
9   Look through everything you've written, whether as text or notes, and try to organise it into sections where each section includes a main idea relating to the development of your overall argument or exposition.
10 Start from the beginning again, writing up your sections.
11 Make sure that your sections are linked and not just a sequence of separate sections. Each paragraph must follow on smoothly from the one before (see Chapter 5).
12 When you think you've finished, check for any gaps in the argument, missing words, typos, etc., then leave it for a couple of days.

13 A couple of days later, go carefully through what you've written again, possibly changing the wording here and there, but sticking to the overall structure (unless of course you spot a logical flaw at some point).

14 ^{ascertain} If you do spot a major flaw, so that you need to spend more time getting it right, ask for an extension of the deadline. You are so near ^{negotiate} to writing a good assignment, don't throw the opportunity away.

15 Only hand in when you are completely satisfied that you've done the best you can.

The Reinforcement Principle

Behind the above procedure of getting to the stage of handing in a written assignment, is an approach to learning that revolves around reinforcement. Points 3–5, 7, 8, 10 and 13 all illustrate reinforcement. Reinforcing your understanding of arguments by associating them with illustrative examples, reinforcing your memory of details by trying to recall them first and checking them afterwards, and reinforcing your ability to recall what you want to recall by going through it at least once again after a suitable interval of time.

The reinforcement principle applies to other kinds of assignment also, such as multiple-choice questions or short-answer paragraphs. These assignments are likely to have been set to make sure you know relevant facts or details and the differences between subtle distinctions.

Multiple-choice questions are likely to be set in test situations in class, but you should prepare yourself for them rather than rely on guesswork. If you have prepared yourself well for a multiple-choice test, you are in a good position to use what you learn in other contexts as well.

While multiple-choice questions require you to *recognise* rather than *formulate* definitions, procedures, or subtle distinctions, as is the case with short-answer paragraphs, the strategies are similar.

Try the following procedure:

1 Read through definition, procedure, or text, once in full concentration.
2 Put the book or notes away and go through the details in your head or write them down.
3 Check that you are right by reading through again.
4 Note any area or detail you got wrong.

5 A couple of days later, try and go through the whole thing again, without looking anything up.
6 Look up what you haven't remembered and to check that you are right.
7 Write out the final version.

SUMMARY

This chapter has emphasised the importance of *thinking ahead* in managing your time for assignments and in your use of the library. It has also pointed to the need to *avoid delaying tactics* – for example, photocopying material to read at a later date rather than reading now.

Discussion of the strategies suggested highlights the importance of *taking risks* in order to become a more effective learner and also the principle of *reinforcement* in learning. Reinforcement in learning includes:

➢ Starting from what you know or what you think you know.
➢ Checking back to see if you're right (thereby reinforcing your original understanding).
➢ Learning from the shock of finding out, when you check, that what you thought you knew wasn't the case!
➢ Expanding what you know by further reading, further supporting examples, and generally understanding a wider context.
➢ Integrating anything that you've learned from feedback on one assignment of a particular type into the next assignment of the same type that you do, in order to get better at it.
➢ Trying out different ways of making notes to see what works best for you.
➢ Maintaining a filing system so that you can keep things together and find them again easily.

5

Getting to Grips with the Essay

warm-up exercise
Look at the following quotes from students talking about essays they've
done. What do they tell you about what's important about essays?

I don't really know what she wanted.

I got quite a good mark for that essay – but I've no idea why.

You don't really know what they want you to say. You could so easily
go off on the wrong tack.

Discussion

The essay is a particularly widespread means of assessing students' understanding. Most disciplines and programmes of study are likely to require at
least some essays from you. It is therefore important for you to get to grips
with the essay, what its purpose is, what its criteria for assessment are, and
how you should best approach the kinds of tasks it demands of you.

However, as the above quotes show, there is often a good deal of confusion over what is required in an essay and what makes for a 'good' essay.

I hope that this chapter will give you a better understanding of the essay as
an academic genre and a greater awareness of how to tackle the essays
you have to do. In conjunction with this chapter, you should also read
Chapter 9 on finding your own academic voice, as that looks at some more
of the particular textual issues that occur in the writing process.

GETTING TO GRIPS WITH ESSAY TITLES

Look at the following essay title:

> Have the causes of poverty in Britain changed over the course of the twentieth century?

This question has a simple yes/no form. However, it is by no means a simple question. You can't just answer 'yes' or 'no' because essay questions are not simply questions that you might ask face-to-face, they are intended to make you demonstrate what you know on the subject and arrange that knowledge and understanding into an *argument*. The title basically tells you how to frame your argument. This frame, however, may be more or less explicitly stated. One student obviously had difficulty with it, as the tutor's comments under the 'structure' section of the feedback sheet show:

> Use the essay title, and, in particular, the *task* it sets you, to plan the structure of your essay. This one expects you to:
>
> a) Analyse the causes of poverty at the beginning of the century
> b) Analyse the causes now
> c) Discuss the similarities and differences

The key words are 'over the course of the twentieth century' but the main point of the essay is only implicit. You are not explicitly told to *discuss the similarities and differences.* As the student in this case was a first-year student and this was his first essay, he was not heavily penalised, and in fact the tutor was very encouraging about his work. What this example shows, however, is that essay titles have assumptions built into them about what is expected of the writer, that a beginning student and a beginning essay writer might not know about. You need to understand what the assumptions of the essay are in order to be able to cope well with them.

TASK 5.1

In the following list of essay titles, think about which words tell you how the essay should be structured. Try and relate the question type to the kind of thing that might be asked in one or other of your courses.

1 What was the Enlightenment, and how have the central ideas of the Enlightenment shaped the discipline of sociology?
2 To what extent does the work of Marcel Breuer exemplify the aesthetics and ideologies of modernism?
3 There is no division in a postmodern society between high and popular culture. Discuss.
4 Reconstruct autobiographically one journey of your own, and demonstrate its cultural significance.
5 What are the factors to take into consideration when starting up a small business, and why do you think they are important?

Discussion

Question 1 is explicitly in two parts. The first part asks 'what' and the second part asks you to relate the 'what' (namely a period in history known as the Enlightenment) to the discipline of sociology. The relationship part of the question is signalled by the word 'how' and by the tense of the verb, namely 'have shaped'. This tense, known as the present perfect, expresses a relationship between the past and the present. As in the question about the cases of poverty, time then and time now are involved. The issue here is not one of comparison and contrast, however, but one of cause and effect. The Enlightenment is the cause, or at least a cause, and the discipline of sociology is the effect. You would have to bear that relationship in mind as you were developing the essay, as that would help you keep your bearings in what could otherwise be a very wide-ranging topic.

In question 2 you would have to analyse modernism as a movement in terms of the ideologies running through it. You would then have to show how those ideologies appeared or conflicted or caused problems for the work, whatever the case may be, in relation to the particular artist concerned. The 'to what extent' part of the question needs you to think in terms of how central or how marginal the artist's work was to the issues of modernism, and whether, for example, the artist was not only a modernist but belonged partly to an earlier, or prefigured a later, era. You would need to give a number of different examples from Breuer's work, choosing them in order to illustrate specific points.

Question 3 takes the very common form of a definite proposition or statement and then the stark instruction: 'discuss'. This little word causes a lot of people a lot of problems, not least because 'discussion' is first and foremost associated with speaking. You might discuss with some friends or with your family where to go on holiday, or what film to go and see that evening, but that is a very different kind of discussion from what is required in an essay. The word 'discuss' in the essay context is usually a short way of saying: 'discuss in relation to how the issues have been framed in the course'. You need to think of arguments for the case, which writers have put them, and which writers have argued against them.

At the outset of an essay on this question, you would have to show your reader that you understood what was meant by 'high' and 'popular' culture and why they were an issue in the context of the notion of a 'post-modern' society. This kind of detail is what is known as *defining your terms*.

It often causes problems for students because, of course, the person who has set the question, their lecturer, knows what the issues are and so it is easy for a student to write with that assumption in mind. The assumption in the student's mind runs something like this:

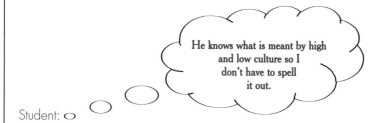

Student:

The lecturer, on the other hand, thinks:

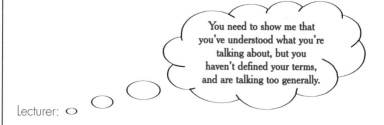

Lecturer:

This relates also to the section below on 'addressing your reader'.

Question 4 is an example of the contemporary concern to get learners to relate their own experience to what they are learning. Such questions give you, the student, a wide range of choice but are just as demanding as the more constrained framework offered by specific reference points such as high and popular culture in the previous question. In this question, you will need to show that you have a sound understanding of 'culture' as it has been discussed in your course, and situate your own experience within the issues raised. Such questions arguably allow more creativity to the writer and give more enjoyment to the reader, as here they are reading something 'new'.

Question 5 again is in two parts. On the one hand, it invites a list or an outline of specific factors and then asks you to evaluate them, that is, to give reasons why they are important or not so important. Such reasons might cover a wide range of issues, such as legal requirements, economic constraints, and specific factors that relate to specific kinds of business. You would have to show an awareness of all relevant issues. Such a question might also implicitly require some comparison and contrast between the factors. For example, X might be more important in certain situations than Y.

From the above discussion of the questions, it is clear that there are a wide range of different tasks involved. These include:

➢ analysis of the relevant issues;
➢ comparison and contrast;
➢ the definition of terms;
➢ discussion (usually involving pro and contra arguments);
➢ illustrating arguments with relevant examples.

Before you begin either the writing or any preliminary research for the question, you must always ask yourself:

➢ What is the task this essay title is setting?
➢ How many parts are there to it?
➢ What is implicit in the question as well as explicit?

ASSESSMENT CRITERIA

Before looking at some typical assessment criteria for essays, do the following task to help you think about what is involved.

TASK 5.2

What kinds of things do you think your assessment is based on?

Assessment based on	Yes	No
1 Your ability to regurgitate ideas, arguments, or details that you have read about or heard about in lectures		
2 Your ability to engage with ideas, arguments, or topics that you have read about or heard about in lectures		
3 Your ability to remember complex details		
4 Your ability to show that you have understood what your course has been about		
5 Your ability to apply what you have read or heard about to new problem situations		
6 Your ability to assimilate a range of ideas and express them clearly		
7 Your ability to spell correctly		
8 Your ability to write grammatically correct sentences		

Discussion

I think it's likely that most academics working in the British context will look favourably on points 2, 4, 5 and 6. The other points are also relevant, but only in association with or as sub-aspects of the other points. Take point 1, for example. In some educational cultures, it is important to be able to show that you have read and are able to reproduce certain material, and in such situations a lot of stress is put on having a good memory and in organising your material in a memorable way so that you can reproduce it. However, as you might have guessed from the use of the word 'regurgitate', which is slightly derogatory, this is frowned upon in the British context. It's not enough just to reproduce what you have read, you need also to show that you have understood it. This implies that you can manipulate the material, take it out of the context in which you first read it and apply it to another context. Usually the application is to a particular argument that you are drawing out, but it might also be to solving a problem. This is why the word 'apply' in point 5 is so important.

Similarly, the word 'engage' in point 2 is also crucial. It assumes that you will take a questioning attitude to what you are reading about rather than just trying to remember it. This can be shown in your assignments by how you link the material you read with the arguments you put forward or address, whether you use the material to make comparisons with other material or perhaps bring in examples from your own experience to illustrate, validate or question an argument put forward in the literature you have been required to read.

ascertain

C

critical

Points 7 and 8 are important, but are usually not what the assignment has been designed to assess. Rather, they are a taken-for-granted aspect of written work in the academic context (see also Chapter 10).

five

69

Figure 5.1 shows two examples of an assessment sheet for academic essays where the assessment criteria are used as sub-headings for comments from your tutor. Most departments nowadays issue such feedback or assessment sheets along with marked course work. They vary a little in the wordings used and in the headings they refer to. However, there are some fairly standard criteria. Both examples in Figure 5.1 refer to the following criteria:

➢ structure;
➢ clarity of thought;
➢ evidence of reading;
➢ coherence of argument;
➢ presentation.

All of these criteria interrelate, particularly in an essay assignment, and if you have done one aspect well, then that helps the others. Because they are interrelated, it is sometimes difficult for students to tease out what the differences are. Indeed, it is quite difficult even for your tutors to define each of them independently of the others. However, I'll have a go.

<table>
<tr><td>

X DEPARTMENT
Coursework assessment feedback sheet

Name

ESSAY/COURSEWORK TITLE
COMMENTS

Presentation (Spelling, grammar,
  referencing)

Organisation, structure

Clarity of expression, coherence of
  argument, relevance of material

Reading and use of reading

Originality, independent or critical
  thought

Other comments (how to improve etc)

</td><td>

Y DEPARTMENT

NAME

MARK AND GENERAL COMMENT

CONTENT AND RELEVANCE

ARGUMENT

EVIDENCE OF READING

CLARITY OF THOUGHT

PRESENTATION, STYLE AND
EXPRESSION

</td></tr>
</table>

Figure 5.1   *Examples of assessment sheets for academic essays*

Structure

Structure, sometimes referred to also as organisation, or as structure and organisation, applies to the overall or macro-organisation of your text. The overall structure depends a lot on the framework set by the essay title (as discussed above), which sets the tone for how you begin and end the essay, as well as indicating the kind of content that needs to be brought in in the middle.

Your introductory paragraph needs to relate to the title and to give some indication of what you're going to deal with in the rest of the essay.

The middle is where you develop your argument, looking at different aspects of the topic, how they interrelate but have different emphases, as well as at points that conflict or show different sides to an argument. This is where the necessity for wide reading comes in. You can't just rely on what one writer has to say on the subject (see the discussion of evidence of reading, below).

The end, or conclusion, rounds things off. This is where you bring together and summarise the different threads of the argument that you've looked at.

Essay writing always involves you in making choices about what to put in, what to leave out, which arguments or examples to give first and which should follow, and so on. You will probably have gathered a lot more information on the topic than you need, and you have to go through the (sometimes heartbreaking) process of 'dumping' some of it. Making your selection of material is a question of evaluating its relevance to the line of argument you are developing.

ascertain

S

select &
evaluate

The following comments from a tutor exemplify the common occurrence of a student putting in material which is not strictly relevant. The comments were put on the feedback sheet undet the heading of 'structure'.

> Clearly structured but misconceived. The central section on Welfare Reform is not necessary and could have been summarised in one short paragraph.

TASK 5.3

Can you think of reasons why the student put in a whole section that wasn't relevant to the question?

Discussion

There are of course several possibilities. Here are a few:

➢ The student mistakenly thought it was relevant
➢ The student had read all the literature on the issue s/he included and therefore thought s/he might as well put it in (as evidence of hard work, as it were)
➢ The student had a need for 'padding' (didn't know what else to say, needed to fill a required word length)
➢ The student hadn't taken time or made the effort to re-order the material after the first draft
➢ The student hadn't taken the time or made the effort to re-interpret what s/he had written in the light of another look at the title and what it entailed

Clarity

Clarity of thought or of expression (the two are interlinked) is one of the 'buzzwords' of academic writing. Just think how many times you've seen 'unclear' or 'not very clearly expressed' or perhaps even just a question mark (?) written alongside your text. It can refer to a whole host of things. Perhaps most prominent is the logic of what you're saying – for example, are you muddling up cause and effect, or are you mixing up too many different, but related points, without separating them off clearly enough? The following is an example:

> Personal selling like anything else can take up different forms. For example flying salespersons can prove costly and also detrimental to personal exhaustion and poor company representation.

On the level of organising the argument, the student starts off well by following the convention of making a general statement or an assertion followed by an example. However, things start to go wrong in the sentence giving the example. This is mainly because she has attempted to put too much into the example sentence. Taking things more slowly but also structuring the argument more tightly, she should first of all relate the 'different forms' of the first sentence to the particular form that she is giving as an example. As she obviously wants to criticise that form, that is, show the problems associated with it, these problems can be signalled – only signalled, not explained – at this stage. The second sentence could then be:

> The notion of the 'flying salesperson' is one form, but one which is fraught with problems.

Alternatively:

> The notion of the 'flying salesperson' is one form. However, ...

Other logical relationships have not been spelt out in the student's original sentence. For example, the phrase 'detrimental to personal exhaustion' mixes up the cause and the effect of the problem. Personal exhaustion (presumably caused by being a flying salesperson) is 'detrimental to' what? The individual's health presumably. It may be that the student hasn't fully understood the meaning of 'detrimental to' and has been trying it out. As mentioned in the next chapter, this is not a problem, as long as she becomes aware of the misunderstanding and uses the phrase again at some stage, getting it right. 'Detrimental to' means harmful to. What the student most likely wanted to say was that:

> being a flying salesperson is detrimental to personal health as it can lead to exhaustion.

Furthermore, it seems that the student was in such a hurry to get things done that another problematic aspect of the 'flying salesperson' role was lumped together with the personal exhaustion issue. The other aspect was the fact that 'the flying salesperson' method was costly and did not deliver good representation for the company. This point needs to be made separately. A possible formulation for this separate sentence might be:

> Moreover, the flying salesperson method is costly and does not necessarily afford good representation for the company.

So rewriting the whole paragraph would give us:

Logic	Text
General Statement	Personal selling, like anything else, can take up different forms.
Example	The notion of the 'flying salesperson' is one form.
Signal Criticism	However,
Explain Problem	being a flying salesperson is detrimental to personal health as it can lead to exhaustion.
Give Additional Reasons	Moreover, the flying salesperson method is costly and does not necessarily afford good representation for the company.

It is my belief that paragraphs which do not make the logical relationships clear are often the result of the student not taking time to actually work them through. They know what they're trying to say. It's not really that difficult conceptually, but it does take time to construct as a paragraph.

You may be bored with the subject matter or feel you can't be bothered spelling things out, but you just have to grit your teeth and bear it! This is a question of attitude, being prepared to put in the time and energy to think things through.

Don't rush the logic of what you're saying. Spell things out!

One further word of warning on the logic of arguments. Beware the cut-and-paste procedure. If moving something from its lodging in a different construction, the logic could be destroyed.

The requirement for clarity means that you must redraft and re-edit your essay several times, to get things right. This in turn requires good time management.

Evidence of Reading

Here are two feedback sheet comments on this issue from two tutors, to give a flavour of what's expected:

Evidence of Reading
Yes, but not used well.

Evidence of Reading
You must try to extend your reading for essays. According to your bibliography, you have relied extensively on (one book, cited by authors), and this will not be acceptable for future essays.

Evidence of reading refers both to how skilfully you incorporate what you have read into the line of argument that you are following and how widely you have read. For example, the claims that you make in the course of your argumentation will have to be situated within the literature of the field of study. This means that you will occasionally have to refer to the 'authorities' that have created the literature that makes particular kinds of argument possible, namely the people who've written the books on your reading list. Reference to those authorities can be by quotation or by citation, and there are certain conventions associated with each.

A quotation involves putting down the actual words from another's text in your own text. Longer quotes are indented as a block so that they stand out from the rest of the text. Shorter quotes should be put within inverted commas. In both cases, the author, date of publication of the book, and the page number of the quote must be given. Here is an example:

> People in Britain hold strongly to the belief that television news is a reliable source of information. This belief is based largely on the assumption that the originating broadcasting corporation is fair and committed to objectivity. As Seaton and Pimlott (1987, p. 133) point out: 'balance is the child of "public service"'.

A citation does not include an actual quotation, but refers to the author and the date of publication of the relevant work. In citations you, the writer, paraphrase the ideas or arguments of the author cited. They are embedded in your own text rather than set apart as quotations. Here are a couple of examples of citations:

> According to Fisher (1981), X involves Y...

> As mentioned in Brierley (1987), these can then be divided into two main sectors.

Quotations and citations perform the following functions: to support or extend a claim made; and to introduce a new or related point.

You should also pay attention to how you structure your bibliography (see Chapter 4).

Coherence

Coherence of argument relates very closely to structure, as the arguments you want to make, the different facets you emphasise, the oppositions you draw out, will all play a part in the overall organisation of your essay. As the word coherence suggests, the different parts must fit together and not be 'all over the place', as it were. This again highlights the need for redrafting, as not even the most accomplished and frequently published writers get everything in the order they want it first time. Points are not only made but elaborated, and sometimes the elaboration leads on to another point, which takes you off the main path of your argument. Coherence requires that you keep this main path clear. Your reader must be able to walk along it, as it were, without stumbling. Each section must relate to the next, with the connections clearly signalled, and the text should 'flow'.

The word 'this', for example, can help to maintain the flow of an argument. It can have the effect of summarising what has gone before and at the same time carrying forward the argument. The following possible sentence beginnings give examples:

> ➢ This means that …
> ➢ This suggests that …
> ➢ This implies that …
> ➢ This is significant in that …
> ➢ This is important in that …
> ➢ This is indicative of …

However, while it is useful, it is not a good idea to overuse 'this' as what it actually refers to can become a matter of confusion. Too much repetition of the same construction also makes for an awkward read, like having to limp rather than stride along, and so is to be avoided. You need therefore to vary your constructions, bearing in mind at the same time that you move smoothly from one aspect of the argumentation to the next. Sometimes, for example, this can be achieved by changing a verb that you have previously used into a noun. The following sentences provide an example.

> A political debate ensued about the ability of the police to *reduce* the crime figures.… A *reduction* in those figures would be likely to increase public confidence in the police force but the police in certain areas were having difficulty in gaining public co-operation.

Other strategies for maintaining the flow from one sentence to the next include using different words but with similar meaning to ideas previously expressed. So in the above example, you could use the word *drop* instead of *reduction*.

Moving smoothly from one sentence to the next and from one paragraph to the next is not easy, but can improve with practice and attention to the kinds of language use that make the links. Paying attention to the language used at the beginning of sentences in your reading for your studies, and thinking about how it links back to what has gone before, can help you in this.

Presentation

Presentation is rather a large catch-all term. It can refer to the quality of the actual object you hand in. Has it been chewed by the cat? Did you spill coffee over it? In short, is it messy and crumpled and not very pleasant, not to say difficult, to read? Accidents do happen, and this is a great advantage of doing things on a computer. You can print out your work again. Rewriting everything by hand is much more laborious. Increasingly nowadays the norm is to require your written work to be word-processed rather than handwritten, and instruction is given by the computer services department, if you do not already know how to use a word-processing package.

five

77

Find your information technology department, and sign up for a course, if you're not familiar with using a computer.

Most commonly, presentation refers to grammar, spelling and punctuation, and sometimes these aspects are explicitly mentioned in the criteria. This is because non-standard grammar and misspellings also get in the way of a smooth read, and for most academics are a real irritant. (Such issues are discussed further in Chapter 10.)

Presentation also refers to your referencing, not only within the text, but also in your bibliography. Most departments give guidelines on how they want you to cite things (see also Chapter 4). The important thing is that you are consistent.

Presentation issues can also be somewhat idiosyncratic. Here is an example from one particular tutor, who wrote:

> Beautifully presented. But please do not use a plastic folder for future essays. When you have 95 to carry around, the extra weight is considerable!

The message is:

Think about your reader!

ADDRESSING YOUR READER

What do tutors want?

➢ Evidence of research, i.e. that you've done the background reading.
➢ Well-argued writing.
➢ Evidence that you are aware of the issues – whether or not you personally agree with a proposition is not as important.
➢ Clearly expressed ideas, arguments and information, relevant to your point.
➢ To be able to read your essay quickly and smoothly, without the obstructions of ungrammatical sentences and confused or awkward expressions (see also Chapter 10).

_{ascertain} Essay writing always involves you in making choices about what to
S put in, what to leave out, which arguments or examples to give first
_{select} and which to give later, and so on. Essay writing involves you in thinking about who you are writing for, namely the tutor who is going to mark your essay. This can be quite difficult as there are conflicting assumptions embedded in the task. On the one hand, an essay is your personal perspective on a topic. You are expected to write 'an original piece of work, in your own words'. At the same time, you know there is nothing new you can tell the lecturer, who has introduced you to the topic in the first place, whether in lectures or through reading lists. You do not have the freedom to develop your own 'take' on a subject, based on your own experience. You have to situate what you say within what has already been said. You are not so much an 'observer' as a 'demonstrator' showing your tutor/assessor that you have understood the issues that have arisen during the course. This often means that you have to make sure to write about things as if your reader didn't know about them already. This forces you to spell things out. It requires stamina as well as understanding. It is usually a good idea to position your reader as somebody who knows everything but suspects you of knowing nothing.

SUMMARY

This chapter has looked at:

➢ the general criteria on which essays in the social sciences are assessed;
➢ the importance of analysing and understanding essay titles;
➢ positioning your reader.

FURTHER READING

Creme, P and Lea, M.R. (1997) *Writing at University*. Buckingham: Open University Press.
Oshima, A. and Hogue, A. (1999) *Writing Academic English*. 3rd edn. Haslow: White Plains, NY Longman
Pirie, D. (1985) *How to Write Critical Essays*. London: Methuen.
Redman, P. (2001) *Good Essay Writing: A Social Sciences Guide*. 2nd edn. London: Sage.
Swales, J.M. and Feak, C.B. (1994) *Academic Writing for Graduate Students*. Ann Arbor: University of Michigan Press.
Taylor, G. (1989) *The Students' Writing Guide for the Arts and Social Sciences*. Cambridge: Cambridge University Press.

You may also find the following online material useful (each site was checked during August 2001).

http://owl.english.purdue.edu/handouts/index2.html
http://www.troyst.edu/writingcenter/handouts.html
http://www.eslplanet.com/teachertools/argueweb/frntpage.htm

6

Making the Most of Reading

warm-up exercise
Here are some reading strategies. Discuss with others what you think the
differences are between them.

- ➢ skim-reading
- ➢ scanning
- ➢ reading the first sentence of each paragraph
- ➢ survey reading
- ➢ reading to improve your writing style

Discussion

Reading is not simply a passive process. You don't just sit down with a book
and start reading. Nor do you always have to read a book from cover to
cover. The strategies mentioned above are related to a variety of purposes
and reasons you might have for reading. In the following section, I will go
through each of these strategies in turn.

READING STRATEGIES

Skim-reading, as the name suggests, involves running through a text
quickly to get a general idea of what it's about. It is sometimes also known
as 'reading for gist'. You might skim-read for a quick first reading of a

chapter, or to get an overview of a few pages, before moving on to the next section. You might also use it to browse through a book in the library before deciding whether you want to take it out or not.

Skim-reading can be done in a situation where you don't have much time but want to make some use of the time that you do have. Ten minutes spent in skim-reading through parts of a book gives you a sense of the tone and content of that book, and prepares you for a more focused in-depth look at a later date.

Scanning is a bit like looking up a word in a dictionary, only you are applying the technique to any text. You are looking for specific informa-tion rather than an overall idea of the text. For example, you might want to check up on the date a book was published. If you knew the author, you could find this fairly quickly from a bibliography, usually at the back of the book.

However, the information you are looking for need not be alphabetically ordered. You might, for example, be looking for what a particular writer has to say about a particular concept, let's say 'poverty'. You would then 'scan' for the word 'poverty' as if your eyes were looking for a tiny boat on an otherwise empty sea. Once you had found the word you were look-ing for, you would read the paragraphs around it, and anywhere else that the author had mentioned, rather than read through a whole chapter.

Reading the first sentence of each paragraph is useful because of the way paragraphing in English generally works. Important or structuring infor-mation tends to come at the beginning of paragraphs. Books on writing usually call this the *topic sentence*. By reading the first sentences of each paragraph throughout a chapter, for example, you should get a general overall idea of what the chapter is about. Here are the first sentences – or in one case, half sentence – from four consecutive paragraphs, to give you an idea of what I mean:

> Philosophy, particularly the recent French philosophical tradition, has been both a prime site for debate about postmodernism and a source of many of the theories of what constitutes postmodernism. ...

> One of the best ways of describing postmodernism as a philosophical movement would be as a form of scepticism...

> Poststructuralism's rejection of the structuralist tradition of thought constitutes yet another gesture of scepticism towards received authority, and can be considered as part of the postmodern intellectual landscape. …
>
> Poststructuralism is a broad cultural movement spanning various intellectual disciplines that has involved a rejection not just of structuralism and its methods, but also the ideological assumptions that lie behind them. …
>
> (Sim, S. (1998) 'Postmodernism and philosophy', in S. Sim (ed), *The Icon Dictionary of Postmodern Thought*. Cambridge: Icon. pp. 3–4)

The title of the chapter, 'Postmodernism and Philosophy', already sets up some kind of expectation of what we're about to read. The first sentences of the first four paragraphs provide hooks on which we can hang further information through more extended reading. They also make the handling of such weighty information more manageable. Possible 'hooks' from the above sentences are:

⥮ The recent French philosophical tradition

⥮ Scepticism

⥮ Rejection of structuralist tradition

⥮ Broad cultural movement spanning various intellectual disciplines

With these conceptual hooks, you are drawn into the way the author is framing the topic. If you were also reading other authors on the same topic (very likely in the context of researching an essay) you could use this strategy to get a general sense of which aspects were being highlighted by both or some authors and which were being highlighted only by one or another author.

Try this strategy out now with one or more of your own textbooks.

Reading the first sentences of each paragraph might be used as the first part of a two-part strategy, where the second part is to go on and read through the whole chapter. When you come to do so, you should already have a sense of what the chapter is about, and therefore be able to get more from it than if you had read it all the way through the first time. This does not mean that you won't have to reread the chapter or spend longer on some bits of it than on others. This will happen where the information is dense or where the content is completely new to you. However, it is ultimately likely to be a time-saving strategy.

With this combination strategy, you are not only able to engage more fully with the conceptual content, but also get through a book more quickly. This avoids the sense of feeling that you are only slowly 'ploughing through' a book.

Survey reading usually applies to the whole book rather than just a chapter and has the purpose of gaining an overview before beginning any in-depth reading. It means surveying the contents by, for example:

➢ looking at the outline of chapters at the front of the book to get an idea of what the book covers and how the overall topic is broken down;
➢ looking at when the book was published (a recent book might be more useful than a book published over 20 years ago, although a book that has gone through several editions is likely to indicate that it is popular and in demand);
➢ looking at the index at the back of the book to get a rough idea of names of people mentioned and key ideas or concepts;
➢ looking at the layout of chapters – whether they are short and sweet with lots of sub-headings, have lots of figures or images breaking up the text, or are long with dense text (this might help you decide, if you are choosing from several books, which one to take out).

The survey-reading strategy is a good way of managing your reading lists. For most courses, you will be presented with a long list of books to read and you probably won't have time to read them all thoroughly. However, just getting hold of them and giving them a good survey gives you a sense of which would be most useful and which might have good sections on some topics but not on others. You can then plan which books you want to prioritise for which topics.

As mentioned in Chapter 4 on managing your assignments, it is not always easy to get hold of the books you want, but there are inevitably some copies for reference only and all of the above reading strategies come into their own in this context.

Reading to improve your writing style refers to looking closely at how an author has structured his/her text in order to improve your own writing style.

You might want to look at how an author has moved from one paragraph to the next, for example. How has the paragraph begun? How has it ended? Which words link one paragraph to the next? How long are the sentences? How are the sentences linked? How long are the paragraphs? All of these things are important and relate to the issue of 'flow' discussed in Chapter 5 on essay writing, but have implications also for any written assignment. Reading and writing are very much interlinked.

ascertain

I

integrate

RESEARCH READING FOR WRITING OR SPEAKING

Often your main purpose in reading will be as research for an essay or other written assignment, or for a seminar. The section in Chapter 4 on integrating writing, reading, and note-taking for a written assignment gives a possible 15-step procedure for this integration. What can often happen, however, is that you get caught up with the reading process.

It is generally true that the more you read on a subject, the more you feel you need to read to get to grips with it. It is very easy to get carried away, to read as much as possible and to neglect the writing process. As a general rule, you should think about dividing up your time for a written assignment in the ratio of 70% writing (from initial drafting stage through to final editing) and 30% reading. Many students unfortunately distribute their time in the reverse order, take copious notes from their reading, and get muddled. Remember to take your cue from the assignment title (see Chapter 5 on essay titles, for example) and focus your energies on that. This means being selective about your reading.

ascertain

S

select

A similar division of labour applies to preparing a seminar presentation (see also Chapter 7). You need to bear in mind how you want to structure the presentation and tailor your reading to that. The reading strategies outlined above help you to keep your research reading in check.

What might also help you avoid feeling overwhelmed by the amount you feel you should read is to train yourself to read faster, at least occasionally.

READING FASTER

You may not have thought about how you read, but you can train yourself to read faster and in fact training courses exist for such things and books have been written on the subject, notably *Read Better, Read Faster* (De Leeuw and De Leeuw, 1965). There is a lot of anxiety around what you might miss if you read quickly, but reading faster than your habitual speed doesn't necessarily affect how much you take in. Some people even claim they have understood better when they've read faster.

TASK 6.1

Try out the following faster reading technique.

Imagine that reading is a bit like driving a car. Sometimes you are in first gear and reading very slowly and at other times you are in top gear and reading very quickly. Take any text that you happen to be reading, this one if nothing else is to hand, and attempt to read it 'in top gear' for at least 3 minutes.

Discussion

You will probably find that you can do this and you may also find that you are also reading attentively, taking in what you are reading. You will probably also notice an effect similar to how you feel if you've been driving on the motorway at 70 miles per hour and you come in to a built-up area where you have to drive at 30 miles per hour. Once you have been driving (reading) quickly, what is otherwise a normal speed seems very, very slow.

The point is not simply that faster reading is a good way to save time, it is that having the flexibility to vary your speed improves your reading efficiency. For example, at any reading session, you are likely to find your

E
ascertain

engage

mind wandering. Sitting up and concentratedly reading much faster for a bit is a way of re-focusing, and also re-energising your involvement with the text. Try it!

Another technique for speeding up your reading is to take a pencil or simply just use your finger, and hold it over the page. You then let your eye follow the pencil as you move it down the middle of the page. Your eye will 'chunk' the information either side of the 'point' as you move downwards, using also what is known as your 'peripheral vision'. This expands the amount of text you see as opposed to when you are reading in the standard fashion from left to right along the line. The effect is to give you the gist of what's on the page, quickly.

Some readers seem to be natural fast readers while others have to train themselves to read quickly. Others prefer to change their reading pace, occasionally putting on a spurt and then slowing down again.

Reading, Time and Efficiency

TASK 6.2

Can you plot the above reading strategies on a continuum between slow and fast?

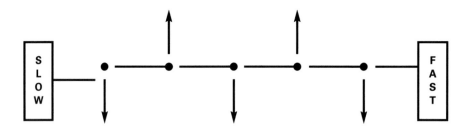

Discussion

There are no hard-and-fast rules about how quickly you should read when putting the above strategies into practice. It is likely, however, that your reading speed would vary according to what your focus was. Skim-reading, scanning and survey reading will all fall at the fast end of the con-tinuum, and this is because of the intrinsic link to their purposes. Scanning is essentially a time-saving procedure, finding the information you are specifically looking for without reading everything again. The aim of both survey reading and skim-reading is to gain quickly a sense of the overall content, whether it be of a book as a whole or a chapter, or section of a chapter.

Reading the first sentence of each paragraph should be slower because of the importance of the information that you expect to find there. While the actual reading of the sentences may be slow, the strategy overall is intended to be time-saving, showing the development of an argument, for example, and the different facets of it much more quickly than if you were to start to read the chapter through from start to finish.

Reading to improve your writing style is the slowest procedure because it involves actually focusing closely on the language used and looking at the connections between the words used from sentence to sentence. This is a very different strategy from reading for meaning or content, which the others are concerned with.

Efficient reading is therefore very much bound up with being able to vary your speed as well as matching your speed to your purpose.

READING CRITICALLY

The above discussions of strategies and of faster reading have highlighted your interaction with texts themselves. While these strategies help you to take a critical stance towards the texts, such as deciding whether a particular book will give you the information you need, or quickly following the line of argument taken by different authors, you need also to ask yourself questions about the content of what you're reading. Such questions could include:

➢ does the author always provide evidence for any assertion made? (you should apply this also to your own writing!)
➢ is there a context that hasn't been mentioned that might alter the persuasiveness of the argument?
➢ is the information provided up-to-date?
➢ is the focus very narrow?
➢ is the focus very broad?
➢ how certain is the author of what's being said (look for words like, 'might', 'could', 'most')

> ➤ does what X is saying contradict what Y said?
> ➤ how is X's account different from Y's account? Who puts in and leaves out what?

It is important not simply to take printed matter at face value. You need to see it in a context. Most disciplines have evolved because individuals have contested other's ideas or positions. It may be that researcher X uncovered one set of data, but researcher Y looked at the issue differently, applied a different methodology, and came up with different data. Being aware of the different theoretical or methodological frameworks applied to any of the topics you are studying is as important as learning any factual information. Being critical in the academic context is not about criticising something you're not happy with, it's about standing back and carefully assessing the evidence of what you read, locating it within the academic discussion it is part of, and showing your awareness of that discussion in your writing.

SUMMARY

This chapter has looked at the major strategies that can be used when reading, both to facilitate understanding and to maximise the use of time.

It has looked at speed-reading techniques and emphasised their use to vary pace, aid your reading purpose, and enhance understanding.

It has also pointed out the connection, as well as the interaction, between the reading and writing processes.

FURTHER READING

De Leeuw, M. and De Leeuw, E. (1965) *Read Better, Read Faster. A New Approach to Efficient Reading*. Hasmondsworth: Penguin.
Elder, T. and Wood, R. (1961) *Harrap's Swift Readers*. London: Harrap.

7

Making the Most of Seminars and Seminar Presentations

warm-up exercise
Take about 30 seconds to brainstorm your ideas on what the function of a seminar is.

Now look at the following suggestions and tick which ones you think are relevant:

❏ an opportunity to practise public speaking
❏ an opportunity to sit back and listen to other people talking
❏ an opportunity to get a better understanding of a topic
❏ an opportunity to ask the tutor questions, more easily than in a lecture
❏ a good opportunity for a bit of a nap
❏ an opportunity to practise giving presentations, which will be useful in job interviews later

---

Discussion

In general, seminars are intended to encourage student participation. For this reason, student numbers are smaller than is normal in lectures. In most institutions the group size will be between 12 and 20 students. The main aim is to stimulate discussion, broaden your knowledge and deepen your understanding of a topic, and offer the opportunity to ask for clarification on any particular issue.

The seminar tutor will usually start the ball rolling, but the mark of a successful seminar is when as many students as possible have had their say. Tutors therefore usually attempt to make the atmosphere as informal as possible so that students feel free to voice their opinions.

Seminars may be linked to lectures, in which case the seminar will pick up on points raised in the lecture and go into them in more detail. There is usually a degree of open-endedness to such seminars and different seminar groups may take the discussion in different directions, depending on what gets said or asked. If you want to make the most of the range of possible discussion, it's a good idea to compare notes afterwards with a friend in another seminar group.

However, not all seminars are linked to lecture courses in this way. Some courses or modules may be delivered entirely by means of seminars. In the next two sections I will look at the two main activities for students in seminars – speaking in discussions and giving a seminar presentation.

SPEAKING UP IN SEMINARS

I only ever speak in seminars if a friend has planted a question on me.

The above quote is a good example of showing solidarity with your friends but a much less good example of getting the most out of seminars. What it points up is really two areas of anxiety that some students feel with regard to seminars.

On the one hand, it can be quite daunting to give an opinion or to ask a question. You may feel that you don't want to show your ignorance or you may be afraid that you're asking a stupid question. These kinds of feeling are really quite widespread among students, but the fact of the matter is that the seminar is there so that you don't need to feel that way, that you can sort out any misunderstandings you may have, as well as try out any opinions or ideas you may have.

Try to make a point of saying something in seminars – doing it once makes it easier to keep on doing it.

ascertain

A The more you hear the sound of your own voice in the middle of a seminar, the more 'normal' it will seem to you that you should be

ask
questions **speaking.**

^{ascertain}

R

_{risk}

Try not to think of other students as being more articulate or more clever than you. This is not so much a compliment to the others as an insult to yourself. You are holding yourself back and denying yourself the opportunity to feel more comfortable about speaking up. The seminar is there for all of you to make the most of it.

GIVING A SEMINAR PRESENTATION

What is the Purpose of Seminar Presentations?

Seminar presentations are a way of ensuring the active participation of as many students as possible in the seminar. The idea is that one student or sometimes a group of students each week presents a topic to the rest of the group, which is then opened up to general discussion. Sometimes seminar presentations are assessed and sometimes they are just seen as an ongoing part of the teaching and learning process.

TASK 7.1

On a scale of 1–5, how important would you rate each of the aspects of giving a seminar presentation listed on p. 92? Put a tick in the appropriate box. If possible, compare your responses with others and discuss your reasons where there are differences of opinion.

Discussion

I will structure the following discussion in three parts, bringing in the aspects highlighted in the table below, p. 92, where they are most relevant. The three parts are:

➢ preparation beforehand;
➢ the live performance;
➢ handling questions afterwards.

Aspects	1 Not at all important	2 Not very important	3 Quite important	4 Important	5 Very important
Doing background research on the topic					
Speaking clearly					
Combining your spoken presentation with overhead projector (OHP) or PowerPoint slides					
Structuring what you have to say					
Maintaining eye contact with your audience					
Timing your presentation					
Answering questions after your presentation					
Reading from a written script					
Making sure you have some water to hand during your presentation					
Checking the room beforehand so that you know that an OHP or PowerPoint facilities are available, and that you can envisage where you will be standing in relation to your audience.					

Preparation Beforehand

Here the most important aspects are the following:

➢ *Background research and structuring what you have to say.* These two aspects are connected because you cannot impose a structure on your material unless you have researched it well. You should break the topic down into relevant sections, highlight the various points that you think are important, and have an illustration ready for each of them. Make sure any facts or figures that you present are correct.

As with structuring an essay, this takes time. You should allow yourself plenty of time to do the reading and thinking around the topic. Also, your initial ordering may change as you become more aware of what the topic as a whole involves. What at first seemed the most general frame for what you have to say may seem less important later on. In order to keep the basic structure of working from the general to the particular, you may then need to restructure the whole thing.

➢ *Preparing Overhead Transparencies.* Here are some general rules for preparing transparencies or PowerPoint frames. Full sentences are not necessary: bullet points will do, and are easier to read. Transparencies should contain the main sub-headings that you have decided upon as you broke down the topic, and any main points associated with them. Make sure the font size you use (if you are writing them up on computer) is large enough to be read at the back of the room. This usually needs to be around 24. There is no point in using the 12 point size as you would normally, as it won't be seen and will probably only cause frustration because of that. If you are writing on the transparencies by hand, do so neatly, and again, think of the size.

➢ *Leaving yourself plenty of time.* Preparing a seminar presentation is another important area for you to practise your time management skills in. Don't leave preparing your presentation until the day before you're due to give it. Your structure will benefit from the time and effort put into it. You will also enjoy the satisfaction of giving a well-prepared talk.

With the 'live' performance in mind, it is well worth checking the room beforehand so that you know that an OHP or PowerPoint facilities will be available, and that you can envisage where you will be standing in relation to your audience. There's nothing worse than spending time carefully preparing your overhead transparencies and then finding out the room doesn't have an OHP, or a screen to project on. Sometimes this situation can be solved with the help of your university's media resources department, but obviously they will need advance warning!

Finally, do bring some water with you, in case your mouth dries up at any stage – it often does if you're nervous, and even happens to lecturers when they give presentations at conferences!

The Live Performance

There are a number of different aspects you need to bear in mind in relation to structuring your talk and how it is integrated with supporting material, as well as how you actually deliver your talk. They will be dealt with in turn as follows.

➢ *Structuring what you have to say and using overhead transparencies or Power-Point slides.* It is a good idea to support your presentation with overhead transparencies if you can. This not only helps you to structure your talk, it also helps your audience to follow what you are saying. Here the integration between written and spoken content is important. You should not just say what you have written down, rather what is projected on the screen should act as a frame for what you have to say. Any illustrative examples or anecdotes related to the main points on the overheads should be spoken. This ensures an integrated relationship between highlighted information and supporting detail.

➢ *Speaking clearly, maintaining eye contact with your audience, and using an overhead projector.* In a seminar presentation, it is better not to read from a written script, or at least not entirely. That is another reason why overhead transparencies are a good thing. They can also act as prompts as to what you want to say next. Moreover, the shift of pace that putting up an overhead, or changing an overhead entails, is a good way of ensuring that you don't fall into a fixed 'reading out loud' pattern, which can lead to your audience 'switching off'.

You should, however, speak clearly. Make sure that you project your voice and don't mumble. It is often easier to do this if you stand up and look round at the other seminar group members rather than sit down.

It's important to look at your audience while you're speaking. After all, you are there to engage them in discussion afterwards. If you look only at your script, the intonation pattern of how you read will be different and you will lose the opportunity to 'chat' with the rest of the seminar group as it were. You can also gauge their reactions to certain things which might mean, for example, that you get an idea of what questions might be asked or what issues might be commented on afterwards.

➤ *Timing your presentation.* You will usually be given an indication of how long you are expected to speak. Try and stick to that time. A well-structured talk, given in the allotted time, is testimony to how well you have thought through what you want to say. The time constraint itself can help you structure what you want to say. For example, you will probably have more information than you have time to include. So you have to make judgements about what to leave in and what to leave out.

Most importantly, you should *avoid waffle*! People always know when somebody is 'waffling' because they haven't got anything to say, and just giving the bare bones of a topic without expanding or elaborating any of the points is very uninteresting and not particularly enlightening. You have to try and make your fellow students feel that they have learned something from your talk. Assume, for example, that they haven't yet read what you have read. (You hope this isn't the case for everybody or there will be very little discussion, but there will inevitably be some people who haven't.)

➤ *Avoiding nervousness.* Try not to speak either too slowly or too quickly. Take a sip of water if your mouth dries up. Try to concentrate on what you're saying rather than the fact that you're speaking. Don't worry if you start off a bit shakily – once you get going, things should be easier.

Handling Questions after the Presentation

It's all too easy to think that your job is over once you've given your presentation. This is not the case! You still have to be prepared to answer questions from other students and your tutor, and therefore cannot afford to just 'switch off' with the relief of having finished!

Make sure you listen carefully to any questions that are asked so that you can give an appropriate response. Again, if you have prepared well for the talk, you are more likely to be able to cope with any questions. You should not have to 'plant' an easy question with a friend, as in the quote above.

Somebody may, however, think of something that you hadn't thought of, and that's OK too. You are entitled to learn something new from the seminar as well. It can be a mark of how stimulating your presentation was that the discussion goes in a particular direction, beyond what was expected on the topic.

Seminar Presentations as Transferable Skills

The value of giving a seminar presentation is not restricted to the university context. The same skills of preparation and delivery are 'transferable', as current educational jargon has it, to other aspects of your life. These include giving a presentation and answering questions on it in an interview and any context where you have to speak publicly. The more practice you can get at university in this area, therefore, the more experienced you will be when it comes to other situations. You may never actually overcome the nervousness of doing any public speaking, which most people feel, but you can become more accomplished and organised about doing it.

SUMMARY

This chapter has emphasised the participatory nature of seminars. You should always try to be actively involved rather than a passive member of the audience. Speaking up in seminars gives you practice in speaking up in other contexts of your life.

Similarly, giving seminar presentations offers the opportunity of developing skills which are more broadly useful to you. These skills include:

➢ selecting and organising material in a way that is accessible to others;
➢ structuring a talk and linking it to visual presentation such as overhead transparencies;
➢ projecting your voice clearly so that your audience can easily follow what you're saying;
➢ structuring a talk within specific time constraints;
➢ building a rapport with your audience through eye contact and a 'chatty' style;
➢ responding to questions on the spot.

8

Getting to Grips with Examinations

INTRODUCTION

It would be very unusual to meet a student who did not find examinations – or, perhaps more likely, the thought of examinations – a source of tension or anxiety. In fact, having to pass a test or examination in any walk of life is going to bring with it a sense of fear or nervousness: 'What will happen if I don't pass? What will people think of me?' Such anxieties are very common, whether they are actually expressed or not. It would be very difficult to completely get rid of such feelings, and that is not what is suggested in this chapter. However, you can help yourself to make the examination process more bearable by taking into consideration how you prepare for them and by putting them into perspective.

It is highly unlikely that you will be in a situation where how well you do in your examinations is the be-all and end-all of getting a degree. Examinations are important, but in most universities nowadays they are not the only means by which you are assessed. The work you do throughout your course also counts towards your degree.

The first thing you must do is find out exactly how you are assessed throughout your degree and how your degree results are awarded. The kinds of questions you should ask are:

➢ How much of each year's or each semester's work is assessed by coursework?
➢ How much is assessed by examination?

> ➤ What is the weighting between assessed course work and examinations?
> ➤ How much does each year's/semester's overall mark contribute to the final assessment?

Assessment procedures can be quite complicated and differ from institution to institution, so it is important to make sure you understand them.

Read your course handbook carefully and check with your personal tutor or director of studies, so that you fully understand how the assessment process works. Don't just rely on what fellow students say.

The process of taking examinations is, like everything else in the study process, something that you become more familiar with. The number of examinations you have to take will vary from course to course and from institution to institution, but what you can do is *get better at doing them*!

Look at your first examination as a trial run for future examinations. Think about what you could have or should have done better. Here I'm not thinking of how you could have answered a particular question better, as that question won't happen again. I'm thinking more about the practicalities or procedures of question answering while you're in the examination room (see more on this below) and preparing for the questions beforehand. Were they the kinds of questions you were expecting? What more could you have done to be better prepared? Did you answer all the questions you were supposed to answer? Did you get the timing of the questions right?

PREPARING FOR EXAMINATIONS

TASK 8.1

What do you do to prepare for exams? Put a tick in the yes or no box next to the following strategies.

Predicting What Will Come Up

The notion of 'predicting' has connotations of looking into a crystal ball, but that is actually not the best way of thinking about what's likely to be

Strategies	Yes	No
1 Try to anticipate the kinds of questions you are likely to get		
2 Look at the papers from the previous year/semester		
3 Go through all of your notes from lectures and from your reading on the course		
4 Have a good night's sleep before the exam		
5 Have a good night's sleep before the exam and hope for the best		
6 Look at the papers from at least the last three times that a particular exam has been set		
7 Think about what questions you would have answered in the previous paper		
8 Write the answer to a question from a previous paper under timed conditions		
9 Write the answer to several different questions under timed conditions		
10 Make notes of the kinds of things you would have included in your answer if you'd been doing the exam paper		
11 Write out a full answer to the paper		

in the exam. It's not just a question of pot luck. You can get a fairly good idea of what's going to be in it, if not the exact wordings of questions. There are a number of factors that can help you to make judgements on what could come up, such as:

➢ What's been covered on the course? Have some topics been given more attention than others?
➢ Look at the course outline you were probably given at the beginning of the course. If you weren't given one, you could ask for one or ask the tutor to

go through the list of topics for you so that you can see how the course hangs together. The individual topics mentioned will be the sources for the questions. Sometimes, aspects can be combined in one question.

➢ What has always tended to be in past papers?

➢ Was there anything covered in the course this time that has never been a topic in a past paper? (It might be a new topic and therefore definitely likely to be the subject of a question.)

➢ Has the course undergone any syllabus changes this year? (This should be stated in the course handbook, but you could also specifically ask your personal tutor or the tutors for individual courses about this.)

➢ Has the course been taught by a new lecturer for the first time this year? (It is likely that s/he will have changed its organisation or given it a different slant, included new topics, and so on, and therefore there will be some new questions.)

➢ Has the course been taught by a number of different lecturers? It could be the case that each lecturer on the course is asked to supply a question for what they covered. If there were four lecturers then that gives you a way of breaking down the possible topics. If there were two, the same principle applies.

➢ What is the subject of books or articles that lecturer X or Y has written? (This won't always work as sometimes lecturers have to teach courses outside their specialist subject – but at least you can find out.)

The Examination Game

Predicting what's going to come up by, for example, implementing strategies such as those suggested above is often related to what is known as *playing the examination game*. The assumption is that you can get good at playing this game, and that it is quite separate from knowing your stuff well enough. One study carried out some time ago in one university (Miller and Parlett 1983) showed just how important some students thought it was to play this game.

Here is an example of some of the things those students said whom the researchers called *cue-seekers*. They were called 'cue-seekers' because they were literally looking for things that might be taken as cues or indications as to what might come up in the exam. They then put all their efforts into working towards the exam rather than trying to cover the course as a whole.

> I am positive there is an examination game. You don't learn certain facts for instance, you don't take the whole course, you go and look at the

examination papers and you say 'looks as though there have been four questions on a certain theme this year, last year the professor said that the examination would be much the same as before', so you excise a good bit of the course immediately, say I'm going to concentrate on four or five topics, the main ones to begin with – and there you are!

(Miller and Parlett, 1983: 60)

The technique involves knowing what's going to be in the exam and how it's going to be marked. You can acquire these techniques from sitting in the lecturer's class, getting ideas from his point of view, the form of his notes, and the books he has written – and this is separate to picking up the actual work content.

(Miller and Parlett, 1983: 61)

Here is a student who is not playing the game so confidently and knowingly, although he is aware there is a 'game'. The researchers labelled students like him 'cue-conscious' rather than cue-seekers.

There is definitely an exam technique but I am not really sure what it consists of ... Identifying the technique is what you are here to do ... something to do with taking exams in your stride ... it's important to have a card index in your mind ... writing neatly, not having too many crossings out so that the examiner likes your paper.

(Miller and Parlett, 1983: 61)

Finally, here are some quotes from the kinds of things that the majority of students said. The researchers labelled such students 'cue-deaf'. These students did not believe that there was an examination game that you could learn to play and play well. They therefore were not receptive to ways in which they could revise selectively for topics that they felt sure would come up.

I don't choose questions for revision – I don't feel confident if I only restrict myself to certain topics.

I will try to revise everything. Exam questions are deadly secret.

I am a very poor question-spotter. What I think will come up, invariably doesn't, so I just go through everything I can. On the morning of the exam I concentrate on the subjects I think will come up – but invariably I am wrong.

> The staff must formulate questions in such a way as to make you show up your work.
>
> (Miller and Parlett, 1983: 63)

The main distinguishing feature between the so-called 'cue-seekers' and the 'cue-deaf' was that the former had a professionalised attitude towards examinations. They didn't see it as being a question of luck as to which questions came up, but of technique. This technique was something you applied consciously to finding out the sorts of things likely to come up in the exam, and then refined by rigorously practising writing answers to those questions you had identified. The so-called 'cue-deaf', on the other hand, did not have any particular examination strategies other than possibly working hard. They seem to lack confidence in themselves. They also seem to think they are in a situation which is outside of their control.

It is these attitudes of the majority of students in this study that I would urge you to try and get rid of, if you feel any association with them yourself. It is against the philosophy of independent learning and taking control of your own study process that I espoused at the beginning of this book. You can change the approach you take to things. Perhaps you only needed me to tell you that!

In looking at the degree results of the students taking part in the Miller and Parlett study, it was found that the cue-seekers, who were in the minority, got firsts although one got a lower second and that the cue-conscious got mostly upper seconds although one got a first. Only one hard-working but 'cue-deaf' student got an upper second.

While it is impossible to generalise from one study of a group of students at one university which took place over 20 years ago, it's worth emphasising the proactive attitude of those who got good results and the fact that the majority seemed to think their fate was in the hands of the gods, as it were, and there was nothing they could do to try and influence it.

There are a number of principles that can be drawn from this study that it is worth you putting into practice. They are:

➤ It's worthwhile revising selectively, rather than trying to cover everything.
➤ It's worth putting a bit of effort into thinking about what questions are likely to come up. It's not a question of random question-spotting, but of reasoned question-spotting.
➤ You should be thinking about what topics are going to be examined right from the start of the course (look again at the strategies suggested for predicting examination questions above).

Going back to the point I made earlier about getting better at examinations, you should begin trying out these exam preparation techniques from your very first examination.

Using Past Papers

Probably the most important thing you can do in preparing for examinations is look back at past papers. There's nothing like putting yourself in the position of doing the exam before you're actually doing it! Your library will have a copy of previous papers on a subject which you can make a copy of for yourself. In such a case, it would make sense to team up with a friend and get a different set of exam papers each. You could then swap them, getting two lots for the price (in terms of both time and money) of one! Many libraries also now offer this facility on line, which means you can download such papers. I suggest you look at three sets at least.

Having got hold of previous papers, what do you do with them? Here are some suggestions.

➤ See which topics have come up more than once over the three papers.
➤ Are the questions very different each time? It may be that they are differently phrased, but asking pretty much the same thing.
➤ Look carefully at how many sections the papers are divided into. Issues of format tend not to change much from year to year, and so you can use past papers as a basis for analysis of the types of question that come up in each section.
➤ Write out at least as many questions as you are required to actually write in the exam. In fact, it is preferable to write out one more question than is required in the exam. If you have to write three questions in the exam, then do four questions from the previous papers, at least one from each. Make sure that you choose topics that are diverse, not ones that are more or less on the same subject.

REVISION STRATEGIES

The idea of *getting down to some serious revision* probably means for most of you that you get all your notes in order and start going through them. You may intend to do textbooks next and then perhaps read over your essays. You may feel good about doing all this, thinking to yourself how organised you are and how you're going to spend a day each on all of your subjects and then start to go through them again. However, this is not always the best use of your time. You're probably going to reach a stage where you find that the ideal has collapsed and you're not going to be able to cover as much as you'd hoped you'd be able to. Furthermore, you're probably not going to be able to do things as thoroughly as you wanted to.

The disadvantages of thinking in terms of such general revision are:

➤ that you might feel psychologically swamped by the fact that you have a vast undifferentiated 'everything' to cover;
➤ that you might feel tempted to flit about from one thing to the next, without fully going into anything;
➤ that the process seems never-ending.

Revising Selectively

Revising selectively means that you are *targeting* your learning. For example, as you identify areas that you don't know enough about you can apply *scan-reading* techniques to find the appropriate sections of books

ascertain where you need to read more closely, rather than read through a book

T because you are thinking in more general terms of 'going over things

target again'.

Working back from questions in past papers can be a good way of organising your revision. You can make this selective by choosing a number of different questions to work on and eventually write out. How many questions you work on will depend on how many you need to answer in the question (one more than the number you need to answer, as mentioned below). If the question paper is divided into sections, you need to find a way of describing how the questions in each section differ. Here are some questions you could ask, to help you do this:

➢ Are some questions more practice-based and some more theory-based?
➢ Are some questions more general and some more thematic or specific to an individual tutor?
➢ Do the sections relate to different parts of the course?
➢ Do some topics lend themselves to questions which could fall in either section? In this case, you should revise for any such questions with that possibility in mind.
➢ Are other topics restricted to one particular section?

This procedure helps you to understand how the examination paper is organised and gives you a background against which to plan your revision. If your examination paper requires you to answer three questions, then you should prepare four questions thoroughly. If you choose topics that are diverse enough, that is, not more or less on the same subject, you should be OK.

Writing Up an Examination Question

Writing up a question from a previous exam paper is a very good selective revision strategy. You are working towards a definite goal, and one which entails doing a lot of useful work to get to that point. It is also something that is achievable, rather than something that stretches into the distance. 'Oh, by the time it gets to the week before the examination, I'll be on my third revision of this topic.' Well, yes. Perhaps!

For most people, writing up a full answer to an exam question is not much fun. However, you really should try and overcome your horror and loathing and follow through with this. The benefits are:

➢ You are integrating a lot of learning into one specific task.
➢ Even if the question doesn't come up in exactly the same way (it probably won't), it is still helpful to go through the process of differentiating the different arguments or points of view and grouping them into a coherent pathway through the topic. Having done it once, it'll be easier to do it, changing the emphasis here and there, another time.
➢ It is a task that you need as much practice in as possible. Examinations themselves don't happen that often. You need to be as good at organising your thinking and getting things down on paper as you can be.
➢ You are increasing your fluency on a topic. Having to actually formulate your answer in sentences, in the way that you would have to if doing the

exam, is a good rehearsal for the real thing. It helps to take away the anxiety of writing something from scratch.

➢ You can test your revision on a particular topic once you've done it. In this case, it's good to try writing the answer under timed conditions. This will probably not get the adrenaline flowing as in a real exam, but it helps to make you aware of the time constraints and to keep your mind on the job for 40 minutes or so.

➢ Whether or not you time your writing, you are pre-living the stresses and strains of writing up an answer and thereby taking some of the pain out of it.

➢ Doing it reinforces the fact that you can do it!

Revision as an Ongoing Strategy

The problem with the notion of revising for exams is that you tend to put off doing revision until nearer the exam period. The fact is that revision should be a continual and ongoing process. For example, after each lecture, you should try and find some time to revise what you've written. The issues that are important here are *timing* and *reinforcement*.

Revising or reviewing your lecture notes not too long after the lecture you've attended enables you to fill in more detail, perhaps even summarise from memory certain aspects of the topic or arguments that you heard about, that is, you do the note-making at this point. The reason why this should be done fairly soon after the lecture is that your recall is likely to be better soon after, say an hour later in the same day, rather than the next day or two days later. Your working memory will be taken up with other things, and when this starts to happen you forget things even that you thought were prominent for you when you first heard them. Some people find that allowing 10 or 15 minutes to pass before you review the lecture is better than doing it immediately afterwards. The whole thing has had some time to fall into place by then, whereas otherwise you might be affected by the 'recency' of the last part of the lecture only (see the discussion on primacy and recency effects in Chapter 2).

Reviewing, completing, or making your notes from scratch after each lecture *reinforces* your learning of the content, making it more memorable than if you'd just attended the lecture and forgotten about it until the next week. It is a good idea also to look through those same notes again before the next lecture. This way, you're building up a picture of your lecture course as you go along. You will also be more aware of problem areas, say where you don't fully understand something, and therefore be alert to situations at other times of your course, such as in a seminar or when reading in the library, which allow you to fit things together better. If you don't know where your problems are, you can't solve them!

The same principle applies to your reading and to completed assignments. Complete your notes after you've put the book away and reread your notes from one study session, before you begin another.

As for assignments, make sure you read through any comments immediately after you get your assignment back, and if there has been a problem paragraph, for example, try and rewrite it immediately. If you don't fully understand a comment or what exactly the tutor is referring to, get clarification. Read through the issues that arose from a previous assignment before you start the next one.

Don't put off your understanding until you get down to revising. Sort the problem out now!

Here are some other ways of organising your studies to aid both ongoing and final revision:

➤ *Maintaining bibliographic references.* Make sure you 'catalogue' any book that you read (see Chapter 4 on constructing a bibliography). It's a good idea to keep a card index of bibliographic references, as there used to be in libraries before electronic data storage became the norm, so that you can easily find those details and don't have to waste time finding the book again, for example, to check the date of publication.
➤ *Linking your notes to their sources.* Make sure that it's clear where any notes you have taken come from, including the page numbers of any direct quotes. It's so easy to get notes mixed up and end up mis-attributing ideas and arguments to the wrong person!
➤ *Maintaining a filing system.* Keep any notes, handouts, and so on filed *in date order* (make sure they are clearly dated – write down the date when you take the notes or get the handout) and *by topic*. A system such as the different coloured paper for different subjects, mentioned in Chapter 2, helps with this.
➤ *Managing your time well.* Take a *pacing* not a *cramming* approach (see Chapter 3). If you learn as you go along and generally keep up with your studies, revision will be more like reviewing what you already know rather than starting from scratch.

Find the patience and the self-discipline to be methodical!

BEFORE YOU GET TO THE EXAM ROOM

Here is a checklist of things to do before you get to the exam room:

➢ Work out the amount of time you can allow yourself for each question. If, for example you have a 3-hour exam, and you have to answer four questions, that allows you roughly 45 minutes for each question. Remember you have to allow yourself time to read through the questions at the beginning, and ideally read through your answers at the end.

➢ Make sure you know which room you are in for each exam and take some time to go there and see exactly where it is and what it's like before the exam itself.

➢ Give yourself plenty of time to get to the exam room. Allow more than you would normally allow for getting to the university. You don't want to arrive late and flustered, even if you are allowed extra time, which you might not be.

➢ Make sure you have enough pens, with plenty of ink in them, for doing the writing.

➢ Make sure you have everything that you need, for example calculators and dictionaries (if allowed and if applicable).

➢ Get a good night's sleep beforehand.

➢ Eat some breakfast! You don't want to find yourself starving half way through the exam.

➢ Try and blank out all the hubbub, panic, and nervousness of the crowd around you, and stay calm.

➢ Take deep breaths.

➢ Visualise yourself sitting in the exam room, calmly going through the questions.

IN THE EXAM ROOM

What is good practice? There are a number of different things you can do to make sure you give the best performance you can in the exam. They are:

➢ Take time to read the questions carefully. Don't jump to a topic because you like that topic. Make sure you understand how you are being asked to frame your answer. Answering a different question from the one on the exam paper is one of the most frequent mistakes students make. Tutors can't mark you on the question that's in your head – that you have set yourself, as it were. They can only mark the one set on the exam paper!

➤ Don't be put off by a flurry of activity around you. If the person on your right or your left starts writing furiously, that's their business. It won't affect your performance. Only you are writing your paper.

➤ Don't panic if it looks as if the questions you were hoping for haven't turned up. A closer reading will probably show that there are ways of bringing in what you know into the questions that are there.

➤ Keep to within 5 minutes of the time you planned to spend on each topic. If you find you're going over time on one topic, try and bring it to a close. Writing two questions well cannot compensate for not writing the third question at all!

➤ Leave at least one line, maybe two, between each line you write on. This gives you the opportunity of perhaps coming back to what you've done and adding something or changing something. However, it can also make it easier for the examiner to read.

REDUCING EXAM STRESS

Some of the things mentioned above, such as not letting yourself get caught up in the generally panicky atmosphere of standing outside the exam room, and taking a first look at the paper itself, are measures for reducing the amount of stress you feel. Other means are not getting to the stage in the first place of finding out that there are things you haven't done. Here, time is of the essence. If you've been doing things, including reviewing, as you go along, you're less likely to find yourself in a last-minute panic. Thinking of yourself as being able to exert some control over the whole process helps too. Don't let yourself feel that you are totally at the mercy of outside forces. Try and boost your self-image as a student.

Countering Negative Self-reports

Do you sometimes find yourself saying to others, or even to yourself, such things as 'I'm going to fail!' or 'Everyone else is so much better than me!'? Cognitive behaviour therapists call such statements 'negative self-reports'. By voicing, or even thinking, them you are reinforcing such negative feelings.

What you must do is try and catch yourself out before you actually express such feelings. If you find yourself about to say something negative about yourself and how you're coping, stop yourself. Try and say that you will cope, that you're trying, that you've got a few ideas to try out. You cannot of course change your attitudes overnight. But you can at least try to think positively. This can only help to put you in control.

If you really suffer badly from exam stress, then you should see a student counsellor. It's possible also that your university counselling service runs workshop sessions to help students cope. You should look out for notices advertising anything like this and go along. You will probably find there are a number of different things you can do that can help. Even if you feel you don't suffer too badly from stress, go along anyway. You can never have enough coping strategies!

SUMMARY

➤ There is a link between keeping on top of your studies as you go along and being better prepared for exams.
➤ Taking a more narrowly focused approach to your revision, such as working up to answering a question that has been set in a previous examination, is beneficial.
➤ Exams are not the only indication of how well you are doing in your studies. Keep them in perspective.
➤ Develop a constructive attitude towards exams and take charge of the process for yourself.
➤ Don't panic!

Part Three
MINDING YOUR LANGUAGE

The aims of this part of the book are:

➤ to raise your awareness of the importance of using language in different ways in different contexts;
➤ to look at the system of values behind what is considered academic, in relation to how you think, how you use language, and how you present your work;
➤ to help you understand what's involved in structuring an argument or being 'critical';
➤ to encourage you to be self-critical and reflect on your own work;
➤ to encourage you to give thought as to how you present your work;
➤ to encourage you to pay rigorous attention to detail.

Chapter 9 taps into the psychological issues of how you feel about using language academically as well as looking at some of the conventions surrounding academic writing. Examples of paragraphs from students' writing are drawn on to show the kinds of difficulties that occur.

Chapter 10 looks more closely at the micro-level of written language, namely spelling and grammar. The issue of why such things are important is put into context – their social context as well as their academic context. For example, precision is seen as an important value in academic culture and therefore taking care over proof-reading is important in academic writing.

9

Finding your Academic Voice

warm-up exercise
How many of the following activities are you familiar with?

➢ Clubbing
➢ PlayStation games
➢ Chat-rooms
➢ A part-time job
➢ Picking up your kids after school
➢ Babysitting
➢ Cooking for your friends or family
➢ Sport or sports
➢ A student society
➢ Going to the student union bar
➢ Tidying your room, flat or house

Which of the activities that you do take part in are most different from each other?

What makes them different?

How do you act and/or speak in each of them?

SHIFTING CONTEXTS

Different kinds of activity demand that you do things in different ways and draw on different kinds of knowledge. If you go clubbing, for example, you will know about different kinds of contemporary music, different kinds of dancing, and the different kinds of atmosphere that different clubs have. However, it might be the kind of place you wouldn't want to take your mother. This means that although you and your mother share several different social contexts, there will be others which only one or the other of you takes part in. This applies also to the other students you are studying with. You will have some things in common and others not.

Language is one aspect of difference in different activities, depending on who you are speaking to, what you are speaking about, and how habitual a routine it is for you. You will probably speak differently in a 'chat-room' than you do in a seminar, and be more wary of 'speaking' in either when it's your first experience as opposed to something that has become completely routine.

Language Use in the Study Context

By recognising that everybody behaves differently and uses language differently in different contexts, it is helpful to see different contexts of the study process also in that way. For example, the institutional structure of the seminar determines to some extent how you speak in it. You won't necessarily say the same things as you would to a friend over a cup of coffee in the student café.

Language Use in the Academic Context

Most students feel uncertain about using language in the academic context. There are lots of different reasons for this. They include:

> learning to 'speak' the language of your discipline;
> structuring your thinking to suit the needs of your academic assignments;
> choosing the right words to suit the needs of your academic assignments;
> feeling comfortable about how you express your understanding in writing;
> putting things in your own words.

These are the kinds of things I want to explore in the rest of this chapter.

SPEAKING THE LANGUAGE OF YOUR DISCIPLINE
OR DISCIPLINES

TASK 9.1

Can you think of at least three different words or concepts that you now use because you are studying X (choose your main subject, or one of the subjects you are studying), which you did not use before you began your studies?

Discussion

The words you choose are examples of speaking the language of your discipline. They are likely to be technical terms or analytical concepts which function as the corner-stones of your subject. For example, a sociology student might choose the concepts:

social structure
individualism
agency
nature
nurture

Such words are like signposts to particular conceptual spaces which the discipline is concerned with analysing.

There will also be key people whom you refer to or key kinds of tasks that you talk about conversationally with your co-students. The following are examples of this kind of conversational talk: 'Have you done your Joyce essay yet?' (where you mean the literature essay on one of Joyce's novels); 'Have you managed to get hold of Bilborough?' (where 'Bilborough' means a key textbook written by Bilborough); 'Have you done your recce?' (a 'recce' is what media studies students might do before they start filming in a particular area to find out what problems or possibilities the site offers). You probably don't notice that you're bringing new words and phrases into your everyday use of language, it's such a natural process. Just as every new teenage generation brings a new set of slang words into the language, and you change your own use of language when you use them, so it is with learning the language of your discipline or disciplines. Your use of language to talk about your studies will change as your familiarisation with the study process increases and your learning deepens.

Structuring your Thinking to Suit the Needs of your Academic Assignments

Learning to speak in the language of your discipline – or indeed disciplines, as it frequently is for students on modular degrees – is not of course simply a matter of learning new words. These words themselves have been used in particular ways as the discipline has developed. They are related to particular arguments within the area of study and particular ways of researching it. You can only become familiar with these arguments and the way of talking about topics in a particular subject area over time. As Russell (1991) in his research into academic writing in the disciplines says:

> Though the students may understand the 'facts', they may not understand the essential rhetorical structures: specialised lines of argument, vocabulary, and organisational structures, the tacit understandings about what must be stated and what assumed – in short the culture of the discipline that gives meaning to the 'facts'.

Sometimes the efforts that students are making to get to grips with the 'languages' of their new subjects are underestimated by tutors. Student writers may appear not to be making very much sense, and some lecturers cannot understand why. They forget that they themselves have become so acculturated into the discipline, having worked within it for a considerable period of time, that they take its 'ways of speaking' for granted.

'Speaking' the Right Language in your Assignments

The kinds of assignments that you have to do for different courses are likely to differ. For example, you may have to write a report for some subjects but essays for others. Furthermore, essays for different subjects require different kinds of organisation of different material.

In a literature essay, you will refer to primary texts such as novels, plays, or poems, as well as secondary literature in the form of commentaries on those texts or theoretical perspectives on literature in general. Your argument will have to take both kinds of sources into account.

A sociology or anthropology essay, on the other hand, is likely to be more concerned with empirical data from real life as well as the theoretical perspectives that have arisen in order to understand the data. You may find yourself discussing how examples illustrate a particular theoretical perspective or how best methodologically to gather data.

It is very easy to confuse the different theoretical perspectives that exist and the different ways of approaching data that are preferred in different subject areas. This is particularly the case in modular degree courses, as a number of researchers have highlighted, notably Lea and Street (1998) and Clarke and Saunders (1999). Clarke and Saunders (1999: 70) quote the following example, where a student taking courses in both sociology and psychology brings some of the terminology from psychology into her sociology research report. The following sentences from the student's writing illustrate her confusion between the two disciplines.

> The problems associated with *participant observation* were held constant in the **experimenter's** mind in order to help alleviate the problems.
>
> There was also the problem of defining the **objective** of the study before the research began.
>
> Thus it may be said that the evidence was found to **prove or disprove the hypothesis**.
>
> It was hoped that the **experimenter** entered the **experiment** with an open mind in order to *observe actions within the context of the situation*.

The words in **bold** come from the language of psychology, whereas those in *italics* come from sociology. As the student had been doing some experiments for her psychology course just before she wrote her sociology report, it is understandable how the confusion arose. This emphasises the importance of the point made previously about tying words to their research traditions or the framework of argument in which they are found (see also the section on authority and using 'I' below). It is not the words themselves that are the problem, but how they are used in their subject context.

Given the difficulties that exist around acting in different areas of study, you must not shy away from asking your seminar tutor or lecturer if you're not clear about something. You may be afraid of 'looking stupid', but it's actually more 'stupid' not to ask. You will probably find that most tutors are really very helpful and would prefer that you asked seemingly simple questions rather than remain unsure about something, which might in turn lead to even deeper confusion.

Don't be afraid to ask!

FINDING YOUR OWN WRITING VOICE

Academic writing is often difficult for people because they can't actually hear themselves 'speak' the way they are required to write. They think, *'that's not me'!* This is part of a much broader issue of personal identity. Researchers are beginning to look at identity and academic writing in much greater detail, notably Ivanič (1998) and Scott (2000), and this is good news as it increases awareness of the range of psychological, emotional and linguistic processes going on in academic writing. In this section, I am only going to point up some areas where awareness of the kinds of choices you can make about using language can be useful.

For example, some people think that 'sounding' more or less academic is about using 'big words'. However, this is misleading. Much advice from academics to their students revolves around 'putting things simply'. This, of course, is easier said than done. You need both to understand what you're talking about and develop your use of language so that writing in a conventional academic way comes more easily to you. The following tasks and illustrations are intended to make you more aware of what is involved here.

Getting the Right Word for the Right Context

TASK 9.2

What's strange about the following scenario? One student goes up to a friend after a meeting with their personal tutor or director of studies and says: 'he proffered me some good advice'.

Discussion

The use of the word *proffered* is extremely unlikely in this situation although the verb/noun combination of 'to proffer advice' is acceptable English. The problem is it is far too formal for the informal context of speaking to your friend. In an essay on the other hand, a sentence such as the following would not cause any problems:

the government did not take the advice **proffered** by the international engineers but instead chose to go ahead with building the dam.

TASK 9.3

What's strange about the sentence: 'The study recites to teaching strategies in the Literacy Hour'?

Discussion

The student has confused the word *recites* with the word *relates* or possibly *refers*. This phenomenon is common when students are building up their vocabulary and using what are, for them, new words. It can be embarrassing, especially if you are made to feel stupid by other students or possibly even your tutor. However, in my opinion, the benefits of trying out using

---

new words and expressions outweigh the risks of getting them wrong. If you get them wrong, your reader/assessor will point that out, and you can learn from your mistakes.

Collocations

The term 'collocation' is used for words which often occur together. For example, you might talk about an *advisory interview* or about *acting in an advisory capacity* but not about writing an *advisory column*. Here the usual collocation is **advice** *column*. It is useful for you to look out for these kinds of combinations. In particular, using more formal verbs in conjunction with appropriate nouns helps to improve your academic writing. You can build up your familiarity with such verb–noun combinations by looking out for them in your reading. For example, you might talk about *'reaching* an *agreement'* rather than just 'agreeing'.

In general, paying attention to the actual language of what you read, as well as the meaning, is helpful when it comes to your own writing. Here are a few tasks to illustrate what I'm talking about.

TASK 9.4

Imagine you want to use the following nouns in your essay: 'power' 'responsibility' and 'authority'. Which verbs can you think of that could go with them?

From the following list of verbs, choose which ones could possibly go with the nouns listed in the left-hand column. For example, the verb 'exercise' can go with all three of the above nouns, but other verbs are suitable for some nouns and not others.

➢ **wield**
➢ **exercise**
➢ **harness**
➢ **hazard**
➢ **exert**
➢ **assume**
➢ **afford**
➢ **effect**

Nouns	Verbs		
power			
responsibility			
authority			
energies			
guess			
the possibility			
the chance			
opportunity			
change			

TASK 9.5

Put the following words into the formal or informal columns as appropriate. Match the formal words with the informal expressions that have a similar meaning. A complete table is given at the end of the chapter.

➢ incongruous
➢ harmful to
➢ to free from blame
➢ put forward
➢ advocate
➢ out of place
➢ oscillations
➢ off-putting
➢ to exculpate
➢ swings
➢ daunting
➢ detrimental to

Formal	Informal

TASK 9.6

The following two sentences say the same thing, but one is more conventionally academic. Which one?

1 Since a teenage girl died after taking Ecstasy, more and more people have been talking about how dangerous it is to take the drug.
2 There has been an increased public debate on the risks of taking Ecstasy after the recent death of a teenage girl.

Can you underline the phrases in each sentence which are responsible for changing the tone?

Discussion

The main differences between the two sentences relate to the use of verb phrases as opposed to noun phrases. Sentence 1 employs the verb phrases: *'since a teenage girl died'*, *'have been talking about'* and *'how dangerous it is'*. On the other hand, sentence 2 prefers noun phrases: *'an increased public debate'* *'the risks of taking'* and *'the recent death of a teenage girl'*. In addition, sentence 2 uses the general and impersonal introductory phrase *'there has been'*. This brings in another major dimension of changing tone: whether a construction is *people-based* or *event* or *object-based*.

Look at the following two sentences.

1   One of the central tenets of this doctrine was that what mattered in art was not the imitation of nature but the expression of feeling.
2   The Expressionists believed that what mattered in art was not the imitation of nature but the expression of feeling.

Sentence 1 creates a sense of distance and of objectivity, helped by the choice of vocabulary. Nouns such as 'tenets' and 'doctrine' give a sense of formality as well as belonging to an area of life that is relatively fixed or stable. They suggest something that is enshrined in law. Sentence 2, on the other hand, brings in the people without whom the doctrine would not have existed.

Both of these sentences are acceptable in academic writing but they exemplify different attitudes to knowledge. Sentence 1 foregrounds assumptions like 'this is the way things are', while sentence 2 suggests 'this is the way people have made things'. Another way of thinking about such differences in perspective is to ask: does history just happen? Or do people make history happen?

Such different ways of looking at things are more or less prominent in different areas of the social sciences, and will therefore be a feature in what you have to read and how you are expected to write. It is worth looking out for such 'thing-based' or 'people-based' sentences in your reading, and relating them to the general 'critical' approach of the writer.

Confusing Academic Voices

The following sentence, which formed the last sentence of a student's introductory paragraph to an essay on the causes of poverty in Britain throughout the twentieth century, is a good example of the difficulties facing new students when developing their own academic voice.

> Throughout the twentieth century I can see that to understand the causes of poverty only through exploring the social and institutional forces can we then be able to see how it has changed.

In this sentence, the student is obviously struggling with the more distant, 'objective', voice, his or her own voice, and the group voice of those people who are looking at the problem.

Let's take apart the features that relate to each 'voice'.

1 The *observing from a distance* voice:
   'throughout the twentieth century',
   'to understand the causes of poverty through exploring
   the social and institutional forces'.
2 'My' voice: 'I can see that …'.
3 The *group* voice: 'can we then be able to see'.

Each of these three voices could have resulted in a perfectly acceptable sentence, as follows:

1 Throughout the twentieth century, the causes of poverty can be explored by looking at social and institutional forces and assessing whether they have changed.

This sentence emphasises the logical processes of exploring causes and assessing changes. Note the impersonal and passive construction: 'causes can be explored by…'.

2 I can see that the only way to understand the causes of poverty throughout the twentieth century is to explore the social and institutional forces surrounding it.

This sentence has more the effect of signalling to the reader what is going to happen next. The writer has made a decision on how to approach the question. Finally:

3a Only through exploring the social and institutional forces surrounding poverty throughout the twentieth century will we be able to see how it has changed.

Or:

3b We will only be able to see how poverty has changed by exploring the social and institutional forces surrounding it throughout the twentieth century.

To Use, or Not to Use, 'I' in Academic Writing:
What is the Difference?

To use or not to use 'I' is one of the issues confronting academic writing at the moment. Ten years ago or so, it was relatively easy to be categorical and say simply not to use it. While in some disciplines or for some of your tutors, this remains the case, a number of different factors are changing this situation. One is the prominence of student-centred approaches to teaching and the valuing of student experience that goes along with it. This not only encourages the use of I, it can also change the kinds of writing task required, for example the use of journals, or reflections on your own experience. However, the academic essay remains a widespread requirement on many courses and can cause problems for students. One major problem relates to what I also mentioned in Chapter 1, namely that you are not the map-maker but finding your way in an already plotted subject specific landscape. You have to fit your opinions around what has already been discussed. It's not like discussing a soap opera with your friend, where you can say whatever you like. Even if you're actually discussing soap operas as part of your course, it will be within the framework of particular analytical concepts such as 'real life', 'drama', 'authenticity', 'stereotypes' and so on.

Your Voice and the Voice of Authority

TASK 9.7

Look at the following sentence. Do you think it is likely to be said by a student giving a seminar presentation?

> The main thrust of my talk will be on what I consider to be some of the most significant issues in the study of the body in contemporary western culture.

Discussion

The use of 'my' and 'I' in the above opening sentence could be said by a student in a seminar presentation. However, what comes after 'I' is likely to make a mockery of any student studying at a level lower than PhD. This is because the scope is far too wide. No student is likely to be already aware of the extent of theorising on the topic that exists and therefore is unlikely to be in a position to make such a statement. In fact this was the opening of a talk given at a research seminar by an academic who is publishing a book on the subject. She therefore has the 'authority' to say what she says.

One of the problems for students using 'I' is that they do not yet have the scope or breadth of knowledge that allows them to make wide generalising statements or judgements. As a student, or even as a researcher without much influence in the field, you have to be careful about the width or scope of your claims or opinions. However, this does not make it impossible to use 'I'. You just have to situate what you're saying in the established literature. As one academic put it in response to whether students could use 'I':

> It's OK as long as they say why or because of what. They can't just say: 'I think …'. It's better to say: 'I would argue that … because …'.

One other source of confusion for the use of 'I' is essay titles themselves. Titles often include a statement and then the word 'discuss'. Discussion in everyday terms is something you get personally involved in. You say what you think. In essays, this is also required, but at one step removed as it were. You don't just simply say what you think, as the above quote also suggests. You position yourself in relation to what has been said in the literature around the topic of the essay.

In her research into how students experience essay writing and how they come to understand (or not) what's involved, Lillis (1999) mentions the difficulty some students had with the word 'advise' in an essay title. The assignment required the student to advise a client on the legal issues surrounding a particular project. After outlining the details of the 'case', the assignment ended with the direct instruction: 'advise the client'. At one point in talking about how she should approach the assignment, the student says:

> If I was directing this to him personally, it'd be pointless me saying this and this and this. Cause he wouldn't understand it. So I have to maybe, in the … is it the third person maybe? Not to him directly, not advising him directly but pointing out how I would advise him. Not advising him personally. Should I put that maybe in the introduction.

There was a confusion in the instruction between an imaginary face-to-face consultation and an assessed academic assignment which required the writer to demonstrate what the legal issues were in the context. In this situation, the student has to position herself in two different ways, in an 'I would advise X (the client) to …' way, and in a reasoning way relating to the law, which would be linguistically more distant, as in sentence 1 in our discussion of 'confusing academic voices'.

Initially, it is probably easier to avoid using 'I' in essays (as opposed to learning journals or reports where you're detailing what you actually did) unless you keep it to the framing function mentioned in sentence 2 in our discussion of 'confusing academic voices' above. Here, the use of 'I' is fine, as you are the one in control of structuring your essay.

If you are at all in doubt about using 'I', then it's safer just to avoid it.

In Your Own Words – The Problem of Plagiarism

One of the issues which is very important in academic life is the need to avoid plagiarism. Every university has rules on this and it is worth making sure you know them, so as to steer clear of any trouble. It is not unknown for students to fail their year if any of their assignments have been found to be plagiarised.

TASK 9.8

Which of the following scenarios do you think constitute plagiarism?

Scenarios	
It was my own idea, I hadn't read X's work. I thought of it for myself.	Yes ❑ No ❑
I know I can't write it as well as the text, so I prefer to use the author's words.	Yes ❑ No ❑
I didn't have time to write the essay, but I didn't want to miss the deadline, so I borrowed my friend's essay, changed the introduction, and handed it in.	Yes ❑ No ❑
I downloaded a number of different articles from the internet and did a cut-and-paste job from different sections of the texts.	Yes ❑ No ❑

Discussion

All of the above scenarios are plausible. In fact, they are actual examples. However, they all constitute plagiarism. The first scenario is reminiscent of the argument about authority when using 'I' as discussed above. Even though the student did actually think what she thought without reading X, the fact that X has written about whatever it is, and is presumably on the reading list, means that the student should be aware of what X has written and relate what she says to X. In other words, the student *must* refer to X.

Such situations where a student feels he or she thinks the same way as the author can be turned round to something more advantageous to the student. If, instead of 'plagiarising', the student in the example had been able to provide an illustration of her own to back up the argument of X, the published authority, she might actually have gained marks. This is because she would be bringing a novel example to the familiar argument, and this is always refreshing.

The second scenario is one which sometimes occurs with students whose first language is not English. In many cases, such students are not deliberately plagiarising. They are not aware that they are committing a terrible 'sin'. They are merely reproducing what has authority, and often that meets the requirements of the pedagogical cultures in their own countries. Also, it is more difficult for them to paraphrase than it is for a native speaker and so it is understandable that they prefer to use formulations which they know to be correct.

Again, the third scenario is understandable from the psychological point of view of the student in a panic, rushing to meet the deadline. However, such students are not doing themselves any service, in that they're missing out on a learning opportunity. It's far better to negotiate an extension to the deadline and do the work yourself than hand something in for the sake of handing it in on time. What is worse, students who would do this risk incurring a very bad reputation, which it may be difficult to overcome.

Downloading from the internet is becoming increasingly common and many academics complain that it is difficult to spot the sources. However, it is nearly always apparent when a student has plagiarised as the style throughout is uneven. In cases where a student has actually bought an essay from the internet, (such sites do exist) there is a risk of losing your place at the university altogether. Some people may get rich from this enterprise, but others can ruin their opportunity of getting a degree.

SUMMARY

This chapter has focused on a number of different issues surrounding the notion of 'finding your academic voice'. This is not easy and will take time. It does not change you as a person, it adds another dimension to you as a person. Here are a number of points raised in the chapter which will help you to find your way around academic writing.

➤ The importance of generally becoming more aware of how language is used differently in different contexts.
➤ The importance of distinguishing between formal and informal vocabulary.
➤ The importance of building up noun–verb collocations for use in academic writing.
➤ The importance of distinguishing the kinds of words that are used in particular ways in a particular subject.
➤ The importance of taking time over the structure of your sentences.
➤ The issue of whether or not to use 'I'.
➤ The importance of building your awareness of language use and the effects it has.
➤ The importance of avoiding plagiarism.

SOLUTIONS

Task 9.4

Nouns	Verbs		
power	wield	harness	exercise
responsibility	exercise		
authority	wield	exercise	exert
energies	harness		
guess	hazard		
the possibility	afford		
the chance	afford		
opportunity	afford		
change	effect		

Task 9.5

Formal	Informal
Incongruous	Out of place
To exculpate	To free from blame
Advocate	Put forward
Oscillations	Swings
Daunting	Off-putting
Detrimental to	Harmful to

10

Disciplining your Language: Spelling, Punctuation and Grammar

warm-up exercise
Read the following quotation and think about whether there is an instance where you felt embarrassed about getting a word wrong or making a grammatical mistake. Ask other people if they have had similar experiences.

> linguistic bigotry is among the last publicly expressible prejudices left to members of the western intelligentsia. Intellectuals who would find it unthinkable to sneer at a beggar or someone in a wheelchair will sneer without compunction at linguistic 'solecisms'.
>
> (Cameron, 1995)

Discussion

As the above quote implies, getting a word or expression, the grammar, pronunciation or spelling wrong is not just a technical matter, it is a social matter. Given the self-righteous tone that some people adopt on such occasions, you'd think it was also a moral matter, where correct grammar means 'correct' living. For the person laughed at or put down because of the particular way they've used language, it is also a psychological matter. At best, it is embarrassing, at worst it can lead to a long-lasting loss of confidence.

However, many people, including famous actors and famous academics, often recall such embarrassing moments where they've committed a 'solecism', that is, used a word or expression wrongly, so it is an extremely common occurrence, and you are not alone if it's happened to you!

A 'solecism', as referred to in the quotation above, is basically a use of language, word or expression, that is peculiar only to you, rather than one which conforms to standard English.

Conforming to standard English is a taken-for-granted assumption of academic writing. This means that whatever dialect of English you speak, and this will vary widely both for students and for lecturers, in writing you have to pay attention to things like sentence grammar, the links between sentences, spelling and punctuation. These things are not simply technical skills, they are an integral part of the culture of academic writing. As writing academically may not have been something you were used to before you came to university, it may be something you have to pay particular attention to.

The aim of this chapter is to help you:

➢ feel confident in the way you use language;
➢ feel comfortable with the fact that the way you use language will come under scrutiny, because that in itself is a means of learning;
➢ become aware of some of the pitfalls that occur at the level of spelling and grammar;
➢ formulate some strategies for dealing with these;
➢ develop your flexibility in language use.

The skills you develop in paying attention to language are skills that are generally useful in the study process. They include checking for detail, taking care over presentation, and being discriminating.

DISCIPLINING YOUR SPELLING

ten

131

Spelling is often something you can have fun with or change. Writing text messages, for example, is an area where this is currently happening a lot. However, text message culture is not the same as academic culture, and in the academic context you have to make sure your spelling conforms to what you would find in the dictionary. This means taking time to proof-read your work thoroughly and disciplining yourself ascertain to make sure you always check the spelling of a word you are not **R** sure of. rigorous

TASK 10.1

What is your spelling personality? Do the following questionnaire and decide whether or not you'll have to change your spelling personality. Try to do this in a group or with a friend, and compare your answers.

Question 1

Do you tend to say:

		Yes	No
a	'I can't spell for toffee.'		
b	'I've never really had much of a problem with spelling.'		
c	'It's not how you write, it's what you write that counts'		
d	'You don't need to learn to spell these days. All you have to do is use the spellchecker on the computer'		

Question 2

What do you routinely do?

		Yes	No
a	Hand in work without reading it through.		
b	Look up words in a dictionary to check the spelling.		
c	Simply avoid a word if you're not sure how it is spelt?		
d	Write down two possible spellings of a word and leave the reader to choose the right one.		
e	Make a decision based on whether the word 'looks nice' or not.		

Categorise the responses according to the list of attitudes below. Some attitudes will fit more than one response.

Attitude	Question 1	Question 2
Couldn't care less		
Rigorous		
Complacent		
Lazy		
Sensible		
Confident		

Discussion

You will probably have inferred from the above that you should:

➤ take care over your spelling;
➤ be rigorous about looking things up in the dictionary when you're not sure;
➤ always check your work;
➤ use spellcheckers with scepticism.

Spelling or Meaning

There will be many instances when what you mean in your writing will be perfectly clear to your reader and therefore you could argue that spelling is not so important. However, look at the following words. What is the effect of the capital letters?

sepErate
arbitrarYly
despArate
obediAnce
trYs
predominATEly
definAte.

The above are examples of commonly misspelt words. The capital letters highlight where the problem is. You should find out what the correct spelling is, but the point I want to make is that spelling mistakes stand out, especially when the person reading your work is an academic tutor. The same goes for awkward expressions and faulty grammar (see the next section).

More importantly, they don't only stand out, they make a bad impression. For many people, bad spelling indicates sloppy thinking. This is the case even though the link is not very logical. You could, for example, still be a sloppy thinker but spell immaculately. The point is that spelling also serves a symbolic function. It gives the impression of careful work, not only in presentation but also in content.

It is therefore worth taking time finding out how to spell a word and in every case checking your work before you hand it in.

It is not enough only to rely on spellcheckers. One of the problems with spellcheckers is that you may have spelt a word correctly but it may not be the *right word*. For instance, *write* and *right* are what are called 'homophones' – they sound the same and so are easily confused, but their meanings are different. It can happen therefore that you write 'right' when you mean 'write' or vice versa. In such a case, the spellchecker won't correct you.

TASK 10.2

Here are some examples where homophones have been confused. The first example comes from an article in a quality newspaper (so nobody's perfect) and the others are from students' work. Can you spot the confused word and replace it with the correct one?

Answers are given at the end of this chapter.

1   There are two questions routinely asked on surveys that illicit particularly spirited replies.
2   Due to substantial profits having been made in the areas of North America and Europe, Vodafone now wishes too invest in the vastly expanding markets of Asia.
3   By December complete coverage for the main islands should be in place accept for the sparsely populated islands far from centres of population.
4   Government institutions take a very active roll in the economy.
5   Resent research has shown that not many people who visit contemporary exhibitions are aware of the actual issues raised by the artists and the art works.

6   Women have a traditionally lower status than men and therefore they are very aware of the value of language to raise there status.

7   All four aspects interact complimentary to achieve product success. (Hint: The word here has two problems.)

Putting the Apostrophe in the Right Place

Although it's often a grammatical problem rather than a spelling problem, the apostrophe is like another letter and so I'll deal with it here. People often have difficulty with the apostrophe, and some academics reach screaming pitch when they see it used wrongly, so I'll illustrate its main functions and also one function which it is often given but which it does not have.

First, it is used to *compensate for a missing letter* – for example, *it's* instead of *it is* (as I used it at the beginning of this section). This use of the apostrophe can be problematic in some cases – for example *he's*, where it can mean either *he is* or *he has*. Usually the context makes clear which is meant however – *he's coming home* (he is) as opposed to *he's gone* (he has).

Second, to indicate possession – for example, *John's house, somebody's book*. One difficulty here occurs when the people or things possessing are plural, when the apostrophe comes after the 's' – for example, *the others' work, the students' union*.

Because the apostrophe is associated with the letter 's' it is often confused with the plural form that 's' often indicates. However, this is a function that the apostrophe does not have. For example, an American vice-president is alleged to have told a pupil when visiting a school to spell the plural of *potato as potato's*. It is of course *potatoes*.

ten

135

TASK 10.3

Put the apostrophe in the right place in the following sentences. There is an answer key at the end of the chapter.

1   The rider who was injured yesterday will not be taking part in todays race.

2   He came back after only two days holiday.

3   Lets go to the cinema together.

4   Wouldnt you rather spend some time studying?

5 Hes a great admirer of Dickens style.
6 She goes to great lengths to avoid hurting peoples feelings.
7 She goes to great lengths to avoid hurting others feelings.

Spelling Out Some Problem Areas

One situation where academics may be more lenient when it comes to spelling mistakes is in exams, when of necessity you have to write quickly. In this situation, they can put spelling mistakes down to 'slips of the pen'. However, it is better to get to the stage where it is almost automatic to get at least those words right that you will have come across frequently in your studies. One example is the case of proper names. Take the case of the novelist Jane Austen and the philosopher J.L. Austin. You could be accused of 'lacking rigour' if you don't get it right – after all, you will have seen the name in writing and been able to check it. You could be accused of 'lacking rigour' if you don't match the spelling of the name to the right person. After all, you will have seen it in writing and have been able to check it.

Similarly, when applying for a course and writing to a particular academic whose name you will already have seen in writing, many people see it as a matter of respect to get the name right. One academic writing a newspaper article bemoaning the decline in standards of spelling among students implied that he was not impressed when someone wrote to him as Dr Mullen as opposed to Dr Mullin. The spelling mistake is easily made. It is the attitude that appears to lie behind it that is the problem.

Increasingly in many disciplines, you will be reading works published in both Britain and the United States, and this has implications for the spelling of some words. One well-known example is the American preference for *-or* as opposed to British English *-our*. So you get *color* and *favorite*, instead of *colour* and *favourite*. As this is something that affects academics as well as students – some British academics complain of being asked by their publisher to spell certain words with a 'z' where they would prefer to use 's', as in words such as *realize* – most people accept either as long as you are consistent.

Finally, it is a good idea to pay attention to word endings and changes in spelling when the grammatical form of the word changes, for example from present to past tense, or from singular to plural. Here are some problem areas:

- ➢ endings in -*ible* or -*able*;
- ➢ endings in -*er* or -*or*;
- ➢ endings in -*tious* or -*scious*;
- ➢ endings in -*ence* or -*ance*
- ➢ single or double consonants;
- ➢ unpronounced letters;

TASK 10.4

Fill in the missing letters in the following words. Alternatively, if you are doing this with a friend or in a group, one person can read out the word (having worked out what it is) and the others have to write it down. Look them up in the dictionary to check.

1 flex∗b∗∗
2 occu∗∗∗nce
3 parl∗∗ment
4 a∗∗o∗∗odation
5 reco∗∗end
6 conten∗∗ous (an argument, for example)
7 cap∗b∗∗
8 con∗∗ious
9 conscien∗∗ous
10 monit∗r

PUTTING COMMAS AND FULL STOPS
IN THE RIGHT PLACES

Basically, commas and full stops do in writing what your voice, the pauses you make and the intonation patterns you follow do in speech.

Here are examples of commas in the right and wrong places. They come from the same student's work, which shows that most students do use punctuation correctly, they are just not always in complete control over it. It's a bit like being a learner driver – sometimes you drive really well, and at other times you're a bit erratic.

1 The book jackets, provide a set of remainders and clues, for 'new' readers, about the look of the main characters and the period in which the work is set. The, repackaging, and reselling, encourages a new readership to engage with the novel.

2   Adaptations, however, are valued by those in television as providing a quality product.
3   When adaptations are acknowledged it is in terms of the negative values, of stock attitudes and stereotypes, which are relayed through a popular, though culturally inferior medium.
4   Television is an entertainment medium, albeit one that also aims, in some cases, to inform and educate.

Discussion

The problem in the above examples lies with sentence 1. There are simply far too many commas and they are in very odd places. When the student was asked why'd she'd put them in, she said that that was a section where she'd used cut and paste. In other words, the commas may have been appropriate in a previous version of her sentence, but when she was moving bits of sentences around, as of course we all need to do, she neglected to check for detail. Cutting and pasting is undoubtedly a great help to the writer but can also create added confusion. The bottom line is:

You must stay in control of what you've written.

GETTING TO GRIPS WITH GRAMMAR

Often students are made to feel that they are 'weak' or 'poor' students because it has been pointed out to them that they have 'problems with grammar'. Grammar looms large as a major sticking point in academic writing. This is partly because lots of more general issues relating to academic writing, such as the organisation of ideas or spelling out the logic of your argumentation, get lumped together as 'grammar problems'.

Basically, your tutor is more interested in how well you have understood the ideas and arguments presented in your course than your use of language as such. However, when the way you express yourself in your writing gets in the way of being able to follow clearly what you are saying, 'grammar' becomes a shorthand term for all sorts of problems.

In the following section, I will give some examples of the kinds of grammatical problems that occur in student writing, so that you become more aware of them and make sure you avoid them in your own writing.

Problem Sentences

One kind of problem sentence is the sentence that isn't a sentence, namely one which doesn't have a verb. This is the case in the following two examples.

> The re-working of the 15th century Madonna and child as Foxy Roxy with the interplay of Naomi Campbell and images from a pornographic magazine.
>
> Wide-scale pollution of the environment, a disrespect for humanity and the depletion of the earth's natural resources.

The first sentence leaves the reader waiting for a comment that doesn't come. To be a sentence, it should continue with something like '… is an interesting example of Ofili's work'.

> The re-working of the 15th century Madonna and child as Foxy Roxy with the interplay of Naomi Campbell and images from a pornographic magazine is an interesting example of Ofili's work.

The second sentence is similar. The comment is missing. What we have is three negative contexts but they are not linked to any point. They could be either effects or causes. As effects, the sentence could look like this:

> **Industrial development has led to** wide scale pollution of the environment, a disrespect for humanity and the depletion of the earth's natural resources. …..

As causes, the sentence could look like this:

> Wide scale pollution of the environment, a disrespect for humanity and the depletion of the earth's natural resources **are sources of gloom for anyone contemplating children into the world.**

Arguably, once they became grammatical, those sentences could still be criticised for being 'sweeping generalisations', but that is an issue of the quality of analysis, not of grammar.

The definition of a sentence is that it has a subject and a main verb. Other kinds of features such as a capital letter at the beginning and a full stop at the end may give the appearance of a sentence, but without a clear relationship between a subject and a main verb such a structure is ungrammatical.

Being Clear about What You're Referring To

Grammatical problems also occur with the non-agreement of words that refer backwards or forwards to each other. This can be the case where singulars and plurals do not match up, whether it be the relationship between a subject and a verb or where a pronoun such as 'it' or 'they' does not link grammatically with what it refers to.

Take the following sentence:

> Advertisements have become a big part of popular culture and *is* now a regular topic of conversation among teenagers.

The noun *advertisements* is plural, but there are two verbs in the sentence which relate to it. The first verb, *have become*, is fine because, like advertisements, it is plural. However, the second verb, *is*, which also refers back to *advertisements*, is singular.

Words whose singular and plural form are often confused, such as *criterion* and *phenomenon*, also require care. These are the singular forms, the plural forms being *criteria* and *phenomena*. So you would say, for example, 'This criterion' but 'These criteria'.

The next example does not relate simply to one sentence but to the relationship between two sentences. There is a problem with the word *they* in the second sentence.

> The weaving of unfinished cloth was Florence's main trade. They dyed the cloth (usually scarlet) which was then exported to the East in exchange for gems, spices and pearls.

Who does *they* refer to? Presumably it refers to *the weavers of Florence*. However, *they* haven't been mentioned. Only *the weaving of cloth* – a process, not a person has been mentioned. To refer back to the weaving of cloth, you could say 'the process' or 'it' if you were going to talk about the process. However, that is not what happens. The next sentence goes on to talk about the cloth. So you could say 'the cloth was dyed red and then exported …'.

Integrating your Own Grammar into that of a Citation

Including a quote in your text, especially if into a sentence, is another danger zone for grammar. Here is an instance where it went wrong.

Lyotard describes the postmodern condition as a direct result of 'the metanarratives of the past have collapsed creating a new theoretical situation in which the concept can no longer pretend to control or grasp its object'.

TASK 10.5

Can you find a way to solve the above problem? Take some time to do so before you read the discussion section which follows. As has been a recurring theme throughout this book, you learn best by actively trying things out.

ascertain

active
learning

Discussion

There is of course more than one solution to the problem. The simplest solution would be to say 'Lyotard describes the postmodern condition as follows' and then bring in the quote. However, there is a danger here that if you do too much of this sort of quoting, your reader may think that you've quoted because you found the ideas too complicated to frame for yourself.

Alternatively, sticking to the grammatical construction begun by the student, it would have been possible to say:

Lyotard describes the postmodern condition as having resulted from the collapse of what he calls 'metanarratives'. This has created a new theoretical situation 'in which the concept can no longer pretend to control or grasp its object'.

You will note that the original sentence has been broken down into two separate sentences and what is quoted has been shaped into the student's own framework. This both keeps the structures grammatically consistent and shows that the student has understood what Lyotard was saying, as opposed to just dropping in a quote for its own sake.

The Effects of Disjointed Grammar

Apart from sometimes making what you say incomprehensible to your reader, any kind of disjointed grammar makes it difficult for your reader to follow the thread of your argument. Also, if a reader, who usually will also be reading a lot of other scripts from your fellow students, has to go back and read something twice in order to try and understand what you mean, s/he will not be inclined to give you a very high mark.

It therefore makes sense for you to get into the habit of editing your work so that your reader can run through it as smoothly as possible.

Make use of the grammar checker on your computer but don't just follow religiously what it suggests you should do. Think about what works best in the context of what you are writing.

Working Together

As well as using the grammar checker, it is a good idea to form a little editorial committee with other students and read each other's work. This has two-way benefits. It helps the person whose work is being read. It also helps the person doing the reading as it helps to develop editing and proof-reading skills.

Many grammatical errors creep in because the proof-reading stage has been left out. As has been emphasised on numerous occasions throughout this book, written work cannot be done in one go.

Take time to edit and proof-read your own and others' work!

FURTHER READING

If you feel you have a problem with grammar, you should consult some reference books on it. Your library will have some, and often books on academic writing contain a section on grammar. Here are a few suggestions.

Carey, G.V. (1976) *Mind the Stop*. Harmondsworth: Penguin.
Crystal, D. (1988) *Rediscovering Grammar*. London: Longman.
Davies, G.C., Dillon, S.M. and Egerton-Chesney, C. (1996) *Master Your English: A Complete Guide to Written English and Grammar*. Cheltenham: Thornes.

King, G. (2000) *Good Grammar*. Glasgow: HarperCollins.

Leech, G., Cruickshank, B. and Ivanič, R. (1996) *An A–Z of English Grammar & Usage*. Harlow: Addison Wesley Longman.

TASK SOLUTIONS

Task 10.1

Couldn't care less:	1a, 2c.
Complacent:	1d, 1c.
Confident:	1b
Lazy:	2a, 2d
Sensible:	2b.

Task 10.2

The words should be:

1. elicit,
2. to
3. except
4. role
5. Recent
6. their
7. complementarily (this involves both a grammatical change, from adjective to adverb, and a spelling change)

Task 10.3

1 The rider who was injured yesterday will not be taking part in today's race.
2 He came back after only two days' holiday.
3 Let's go to the cinema together.
4 Wouldn't you rather spend some time studying?
5 He's a great admirer of Dickens's style.
6 She goes to great lengths to avoid hurting people's feelings.
7 She goes to great lengths to avoid hurting others' feelings.

Part Four

MOVING ON AFTER UNIVERSITY

I have mentioned before the importance placed in today's universities on the relevance of their education to the world of work. The issue of relevance is often captured by the notion of 'transferable skills'. In this short final part of the book, I want to look at how the skills you have developed in, for example, writing essays, giving seminar presentations and using the library can transfer to the world of looking for work.

11

Putting Yourself on the Job Market

warm-up exercise
Brainstorm for a couple of minutes on the skills you think you learn at university that can transfer to the job market. If possible, do this with others and compare what you come up with.

TRANSFERABLE SKILLS

When asked to reflect back on their own experiences of university, the well-known broadcasters Melvyn Bragg and Allan Little gave answers typical of independent learners. They emphasised the process of learning and the motivation to learn.

➢ I learnt what I wanted to do with my life. I knew that I wanted to write fiction and I wanted to keep learning stuff
    (Melvyn Bragg – in *Guardian Higher*, 7 September 1999, in answer to the question, What did you really learn at university?)

➢ The intellectual discipline you acquire while studying is at the heart of what you do as a journalist – it is a continual process of assessing information, interpreting, making judgements about what matters, what doesn't and why.
    (Allan Little in answer to the question: did your degree prepare you for the world of work? In *EdiT*, The University of Edinburgh Magazine, Volume, 2,2, 2000.)

University is not just about the content of what you study, it is also about the skills you develop through interacting with content. You can then go on being a learner, applying those skills to different kinds of content in different contexts throughout your life. This is often talked about as developing *transferable skills*, a buzz word with employers and with university administrators. What Allan Little talks about in the quote above as 'the intellectual discipline' of 'assessing information, interpreting, making judgements about what matters, what doesn't and why' may also be seen as transferable skills. They transfer from the process of being a student to being a journalist. You may find that in your student handbook, you have listed the 'key skills' or 'transferable skills' that studying your particular subject or subjects will help you to develop. Some may be practical such as creating statistical charts or tables, while others may be more abstract such as making judgements based on the evidence available.

This book has emphasised the importance of learning to become an independent learner. This in itself is a transferable skill. Whether you continue being a student and go on to postgraduate studies, get down to job-hunting right away, or have the freedom, time, and money to go 'travelling' for a year or so first, the myriad skills of taking charge of your learning and managing the study process should stand you in good stead. What I want to focus on particularly however, in this last chapter, is the process of getting a job.

PREPARING FOR WORK AFTER THE DEGREE

You may have already been in the workplace before you went to university, but you are a different person now and you present yourself for work as that 'new' person rather than as the pre-degree you.

For many of you, the process of job-hunting will already have begun in your final year. Your university careers office will have details of companies to apply to and often representatives from some of the larger companies will come to your university to give information and to offer interviews. Some lucky students therefore leave university with a job lined up.

Make sure you become familiar with your university careers office and the kinds of services it can offer you. This process can begin as early as your first year!

If you're reading this, as many of you will be, before your final year, and therefore the prospect of actively looking for a full-time job after your degree will seem some time off, think about how important it will be at this stage to have done the best you could during your degree. It will be too late if you only realise at the end of your degree that you could have done better.

Make a point of improving your study strategies and your approach to learning now, to maximise your chances of getting a good degree and having a head start in the employ-ment market

THE JOB APPLICATION PROCESS

Here are three of the commonest ways of applying for jobs:

➢ through graduate training programmes;
➢ direct applications for advertised positions;
➢ sending out your CV on spec.

Applying for entry into a graduate training programme such as with a bank, or the National Health Service, the civil service, or the police, is most likely to be by means of an application form that these organisations have already prepared.

The candidate selection process may be held in several stages. After ini-tial selection from the application forms, there may be preliminary inter-views, then you may be asked to take particular psychological or personality tests, and then a further interview. So the whole procedure can take quite a lot of time.

If you fail to get selected for the first programme you try for, don't be too downhearted, pick yourself up and try for the next one. Don't just say exactly what you said on the previous application form, which would have been slightly different anyway, try to express yourself better, and tailor your abilities and experiences as well as you can to the kind of programmes on offer. There is more below on the kinds of questions you are asked on such forms.

Similarly if you get to an initial interview but no further, think of the opportunity of getting an interview as valuable experience.

ANSWERING APPLICATION FORM QUESTIONS

Here are some examples of types of application form questions.

➤ Can you give an example of when you worked well in a group?
➤ Can you give an example of something that you feel you did really well?
➤ Can you give an example of an instance where you felt you could have done something better?
➤ Can you say something about how you coped with a difficult situation?

Try and formulate what you say on the application form in a way that emphasises the skills you have gained through the experience you are telling your prospective employers about. Don't ramble on in storytelling mode, try and break down the episode from your experience, whatever it is, into the kinds of analytical categories that most employers think in terms of. Here are a few such categories to bear in mind (see also the section on linking experience with skills, below):

➤ taking up a *challenge*;
➤ showing *responsibility*;
➤ evidence of good *interpersonal skills* (working well with people);
➤ evidence of *customer service skills*;
➤ experience of *team work*;
➤ showing *initiative*.

eleve

1∕

PREPARING YOUR CV

TASK 11.1

Look at the first page of the three (fictitious) CVs below. How do they strike you as different? Which do you want to pay more attention to?

Curriculum Vitae
Iona Montague

Personal Details

Term Time Address:	**Home Address**	**Nationality:**	British
Halls of Residence	46 Cooks Road		
University	London	**Date of Birth:**	28 August 1979
Kent TN24 0NG	N16 5AR		
Tel: 01234 567 890	Tel: 020 8765 4321	**Email:**	i.mont@y.ac.uk

Education

1999–2001	University of Innovation & Excellence
	BSc (Hons) Business Studies: Courses include international marketing, corporate strategy, accounting and finance, and management economics
	Skills gained: team work, presentation skills, research and analytical skills and time management
1997–1999	Inner City Comprehensive
	A-Levels: Business Studies (C), English (C)
	AS Level: French (C)

CV No 1

Curriculum Vitae

Full Name:	**Timothy George Buchanan**
Date of birth:	**22/2/66**
Place of birth:	**Sunderland**
	Tyne and Wear
	United Kingdom
Nationality:	**British**
Present Address:	**14 Cavendish Avenue**
	Norfolk
	NR6 6JD
Telephone:	**04776 897 990**
Education:	
1996–1997	**Access Course in Primary Education**
	Bramwell College of Further Education
1997–2000	**BEd (2:1)**
	University of Appleton

CV No 2

CURRICULUM VITAE

NAME: Ayse BILOGUN

DATE OF BIRTH: 26/06/80

PLACE OF BIRTH: Brighton, England

NATIONALITY: British

PRESENT ADDRESS: Saltmine Lane
                    Dundee
                    Scotland
                    Tel: 07301 148794

EDUCATION

1997–2000   Badminton University
                    BA (Hons) Fine Art (IIi)

CV No 3

Here is a checklist of points to remember in terms of how you present your CV:

✓ *Necessary personal details.* Usually name, date of birth, current address, telephone number and e-mail (if applicable) or where you can best be contacted.
✓ *Leave out unnecessary personal details.* It is not usually necessary to include a photograph, your marital status, your race or your religion.
✓ *Clarity of personal details.* Consider using a larger font size or different font from the following details of your educational history and the rest of your CV. Alternatively, set out your personal details horizontally across the page, as in CV no. 1 above.
✓ *Attention to layout.* Don't cram things too close together; make it easy for the reader to follow at a glance the information that is being given. Leave one and a half line spaces between each line, and use 12 or 14 point type. Leave double the amount of spacing between sections, and make sure each section has a heading, possibly in bold.
✓ *Sequencing of details.* Work backwards from the present.
✓ *Include grades* with A levels, etc.
✓ *Link work experience to skills gained.* For example, don't just say 'I worked in a flower shop', make it achievement orientated, as in: 'At A&J Flowers Ltd., I developed a creative flair making up floral arrangements, and learnt a lot about customer service'.

THINKING OF YOUR EXPERIENCE
IN TERMS OF SKILLS GAINED

TASK 11.2

Match the following study tasks and examples of work experience with the skills they develop. A list of possible skills is given, but you may think of lots more.

Work Experience	Skills
Working in a pub	
Stacking shelves in a supermarket	
Helping out at a riding stables	
Voluntary work at a sports club	
Babysitting	
Setting up a child care rota	
Giving a seminar presentation	
Studying as a mother/father with young children	
Working as a shop assistant	
Writing academic assignments	
Handling a large workload	

IT skills
Customer service skills
Interpersonal skills
Written communication skills
Spoken communication skills
Coping skills
Organisational skills
Administrative skills
Creative skills
Perseverance

Leadership skills
Problem-solving skills
Information-gathering skills
Synthesising information
Analytical skills
Handling change
Handling diversity
Reliability

The Covering Letter

When applying for jobs directly in response to an advertisement, you may not have to fill in an application form. In such a case, you need to include a covering letter along with your CV. A standard covering letter would simply say something like the following:

Dear Sir or Madam,

NAME OF POST YOU ARE APPLYING FOR

I am interested in applying for the above vacancy and enclose my curriculum vitae.

If you require further details please do not hesitate to contact me. (This is more like a routine formula than something that is absolutely necessary.)

I look forward to hearing from you.

Yours faithfully, (or Yours sincerely, if you have mentioned the person to whom you are sending the letter by name)

Your Signature

Your name in capital letters

The Covering Letter as Opportunity

A covering letter such as the above misses the opportunity to show clearly and succinctly how you fit the post offered. If you are applying directly for a vacancy which you have seen advertised, further details of what is required for the post are likely to have been sent to you. You should use these details to **structure** your covering letter. These details are known as the job specification.

Let's take a look at the following three fictitious posts. How might you structure your covering letter in relation to them?

METROPOLITAN MUSEUM OF ARTS AND CRAFTS

Retail Assistant

The Metropolitan Museum of Arts is a major public venue and receives over 10 million visitors a year.

A lively graduate is required to work in its large, busy, museum shop. Must have good interpersonal skills, broad knowledge of art history, and sound administrative ability.

Could be a good opportunity for a recent graduate in an arts related field.

Job Advert A

MIDDLETON MANOR PRIMARY SCHOOL

Newly Qualified Year 3 Teacher

Middleton Manor is a bustling multi-cultural primary school in the Exminster area of the city. You will have:

∧ Some experience of working in a multi-cultural school
∧ The ability to work well with children from a variety of different backgrounds
∧ The ability to work under pressure
∧ The ability to work well in a team
∧ Flair and initiative in dealing with young children
∧ Good communication skills

Job Advert B

FRESCO

Quality Controller

A quality controller is required to assess the quality of fresh fruit and vegetables as they are delivered to the store.

You will be required to monitor the delivery of fresh produce and make recommendations as to its quality, based on our company specifications.

You will be required to write up a report on each consignment and forward it to your line manager in the quality assurance office.

Initial training in quality assurance procedures will be provided.

Job Advert C

Here is an example of how the holder of CV No 3 above might apply for post A.

Dear Ms A:

RE: Retail Assistant in the Metropolitan Museum of Arts and Crafts

I am very much interested in applying for the above post and enclose my CV.

I think you will find that my experience and qualifications meet your requirements most satisfactorily.

Whilst still at school, I had a Saturday job at my local Arts Centre. I gained a good working knowledge of both the kind of retail business that was done and the kinds of people who visited. I was praised by the head of centre for my administrative ability, my good time-keeping and my open and friendly manner with everybody who came into the centre.

I have a degree in graphic design and my course included lectures on European art history which I very much enjoyed, and I did well in my assignments.

In the hope that I might discuss my knowledge and experience further with you at interview, I look forward to hearing from you.

Yours sincerely,

THE INTERVIEW

Look back at Chapter 7 on giving seminar presentations. The interview requires similar skills. Only the context is different.

Very often if you are offered an interview, you will be asked to give a short presentation on a topic. You should give a lot of careful thought to this, prepare some OHP slides or PowerPoint slides (making sure that you've rung up in advance to request the appropriate equipment) and time yourself giving it.

Usually the amount of time that you are asked to speak for is specified and you should be careful not to overrun. Saying what you have to say in as succinct a manner as possible is always appreciated.

Anticipating Questions

It helps to try and think of the kinds of questions you might be asked in an interview. Here are some things you could do in preparation for this.

➢ Look back at the job specification. There is likely to be at least one question that is intended to bring out the kind of information that your interviewers can judge you on, with regard to each specification.
➢ You should always prepare something to say in answer to the question '*Why are you interested in this job?*'.

In order to answer the above question or a similar question well, it's a good idea to have as clear an idea as possible of what the job entails. Ask yourself:

➢ How big is the company or organisation?
➢ What are its main concerns?

Usually the information on the company or organisation is sent out with the letter inviting you for interview.

➢ Make sure you read this information thoroughly and well in advance.
➢ Don't just find out on the bus on your way to the interview that there's something you should have thought about before!

Overcoming Nervousness

Before you go into the interview room, take some deep breaths, walk in confidently (even if you don't feel it) and smile at everyone as you go in. Try not to be daunted by the number of people facing you, focus on them rather than think about them looking at you. It may help to have visualised yourself going through the interview in advance, rehearsing your presentation or the answers you might give.

Most interviewers are fairly sympathetic if you're a little bit nervous. Provided you have prepared yourself well and answer the questions in a coherent and relevant manner, it won't matter if you occasionally speak too fast, or run out of breath, or have to pause for a drink of water. You may even say at some stage: 'Excuse me. I'm a little bit nervous.' This will buy you a bit of time and you can begin again to answer the question or regain your composure.

In the Interview

Make sure that you have organised what you want to say or show in your presentation in sequence, so that you don't have to scrabble around to find things.

Take your time to get any papers or slides out of your briefcase. Don't give a sense of being in a hurry to get things over with.

After you have given your presentation, take time to sit down comfortably and try to appear relaxed. It might help if you sit well back in the chair rather than lean forward anxiously.

Listen carefully to the questions as they are asked. If you haven't quite understood any of them, don't worry about asking for them to be repeated.

Sometimes, when there is more than one interviewer, the questions can be a bit similar. Try to answer them in the terms that the questioner has used, and if necessary, refer back to what you said in answer to another question, but reformulate that answer. So you might begin: 'As I said in answer to a previous question ...'.

There is no harm in specific details of your experience, or your stance on a particular aspect of the job, being refocused as they relate to different questions.

Bon Voyage!

In Chapter 1, I spoke of the process of managing your studies and deepening your learning as being like a journey. It only remains for me now to wish you all the best on that journey, and the remainder of your life's journey after your undergraduate degree.

eleven

References

American Psychological Association (1994) *Publication Manual of the American Psychological Association*. 4th edn. Washington, DC: APA.

Buzan, T. (1981) *Make the Most of Your Mind*. London: Pan.

Buzan, T. (1982) *Use Your Head*. London: Ariel Books, British Broadcasting Corporation.

Buzan, T. (1986) *Use Your Memory*. London: BBC Publications.

Cameron, D. (1995) *Verbal Hygiene*. London: Routledge.

Carey, G.V. (1976) *Mind the Stop*. Harmondsworth: Penguin.

Clarke, J. and Saunders, C. (1999) 'Negotiating academic genres: The double burden for international students', in H. Bool and P. Luford (eds), *Academic Standards and Expectations. The Role of EAP*. Nottingham: Nottingham University Press.

De Leeuw, M. and De Leeuw, E. (1965) *Read Better, Read Faster. A New Approach to Efficient Reading*. Harmondsworth: Penguin.

Entwistle, N. and Wilson, J. (1977) *Degrees of Excellence: The Academic Achievement Game*. London: Hodder & Stoughton.

Ivanič, R. (1998) *Writing and Identity. The Discoursal Construction of Identity in Academic Writing*. Amsterdam: John Benjamins.

Ivanič, R., Clark, R. and Rimmershaw, R. (2000) 'What am I supposed to make of this? The messages conveyed to students by tutors' written comments', in M.R. Lea and B. Stierer (eds), *Student Writing in Higher Education: New Contexts*. Buckingham: Society for Research into Higher Education and Open University Press, pp. 47–65.

Lea, M. and Street, B. (1998) 'Student writing and staff feedback in higher education: An academic literacies approach', *Studies in Higher Education*, 23(2): 157–72.

Lillis, T. (1999). 'Whose "common sense"? Essayist literacy and the institutional practice of mystery', in C. Jones, J. Turner and B. Street (eds), *Students Writing in the University: Cultural and Epistemological Issues*. Amsterdam: John Benjamins, pp. 127–47.

Marton, F., Hounsell, D. and Entwistle, N. (eds) (1984) *The Experience of Learning*. Edinburgh: Scottish Academic Press.

Miller, C.M.L. and Parlett, M. (1983) *Up to the Mark. A Study of the Examination Game*. Society for Research into Higher Education monograph 21. London: SRHE.

Miller, G.A. (1956) 'The magical number seven, plus or minus two', *Psychological Review*, pp. 63, 81–97.

Northedge, A. (1990) *The Good Study Guide*. Buckingham: Open University.

Russell, D. (1991) *Writing in the Academic Disciplines, 1870–1990. A Curricular History*. Carbondale: Southern Illinois University Press.

Scott, M. (2000) 'Writing in postgraduate teacher training: A question of identity', in M.R. Lea and B. Stierer (eds), *Student Writing in Higher Education. New Contexts*. Buckingham: Society for Research into Higher Education and Open University Press, pp. 112–24.

Swales, J.M. and Feak, C.B. (1994) *Academic Writing for Graduate Students*. Ann Arbor: University of Michigan Press.

Yates, F.A. (1969) *The Art of Memory*. Harmondsworth: Penguin.

Index